HOW TO
LAND YOUR
DREAM
GRADUATE
JOB

From Choosing a Career to
Securing an Offer, We Show
You How to Dominate the
Internship & Graduate
Job Race

A. RAJA

Published by Academic Underdogs Ltd

Printed in the United Kingdom

Cover design by SJ

First Printing, 2019

ISBN 978-0-9933488-5-3

Academic Underdogs Ltd
Roberts House, 2 Manor Rd, Ruislip, Middlesex HA4 7LB

www.AcademicUnderdogs.com

Contents

Chapter 1 Who am I?...1
Chapter 2 Who I Think you Are...8
Chapter 3 What's in This Book..16

First thing's first

Chapter 4 Born-Study-Work-Die? 23
Chapter 5 What Does a Good Job Look Like? 45
Chapter 6 Should you Follow your Passion? 48
Chapter 7 What Should I Aim for in a Career? 57
Chapter 8 First Thing's First 72

Tangibles (Money)

Chapter 9   Does Money Buy you Happiness? 77
Chapter 10 Financial Freedom and why it Matters....................86
Chapter 11 How to be Financially Free in 6 Months 93
Chapter 12 How to be Financially Free in 10 Years 95
Chapter 13 How to be Financially Free in 20+ Years 108
Chapter 14 Hybrid Career Paths...136
Chapter 15 Tangibles (Money)...140

Intangibles

Chapter 16 What you Can't Measure 147
Chapter 17 Start with What You're Good at 149
Chapter 18 How to Find Engaging Work 169
Chapter 19 How to Find Meaningful Work...............................174
Chapter 20 Intangibles...181

The Ultimate Career Strategy

Chapter 21 Iterate your Way Towards an Ideal Career 187
Chapter 22 How to Use PAFC to Get Ahead 198

Pick Your Weapon

Chapter 23 **First Steps**..**205**
Chapter 24 **Starting a Business & Joining Small Companies** **208**
Chapter 25 **Internships, Placements & Graduate Programmes** **225**

Aim

Chapter 26 **How to Find 'the one'**...**233**
Chapter 27 **How to Narrow Down the Options** **237**
Chapter 28 **How to Research Careers Properly** **253**
Chapter 29 **Tallying up your Tangibles** **259**
Chapter 30 **Aim**..**271**

Fire

Chapter 31 **How to Get an Offer in the Bag** **289**
Chapter 32 **Identify Target Organisations & Build a Database** **291**
Chapter 33 **What's Your Truth-Blag Ratio?**...................................**306**
Chapter 34 **What's Your X-Factor?** **317**
Chapter 35 **Starter Questions**..**324**
Chapter 36 **How to Write an Attention-Grabbing CV** **327**
Chapter 37 **Asset Checklist**..**332**
Chapter 38 **How to Secure a Job at a Small Company** **334**
Chapter 39 **Big Companies** **343**
Chapter 40 **Acing Psychometric Tests**..**346**
Chapter 41 **Interview Technique** **352**
Chapter 42 **Fire**..**363**

Check

Chapter 43 **Learn & Pivot** **369**
Chapter 44 **The Ultimate Career Strategy**......................................**375**

Onwards & Upwards

Chapter 45 **How to Land Your Dream Graduate Job** **381**
Appendix 1 ....**387**
Appendix 2 ....**397**

Chapter 1
Who am I?

An author friend of mine once told me that the most important parts of any book are the first few paragraphs and the final few paragraphs. The former, he claimed, should provide the reader with an incentive to read, a reason to stay with the author over the course of 200+ pages; the latter, he said, should wrap everything up neatly, leaving the reader feeling enlightened and encouraged and making a impact that lasts far beyond those final pages.

Every time I start a new book, I can hear those words in my head. So, how can I entice you into reading this, what reason can I give you to stay with me over nearly 70,000 words?

The ending will speak for itself. I am confident that by the time you finish this book you will be ready to change your life for the better and will have all the tools you need to do so. As for the beginning, I think it's best to start with my own story.

It may not be a hard-hitting, top-shelf autobiography. My story is not a high-octane adventure filled with extreme hedonism and last-gasp redemption. But it is a story relevant to your own, a story of discovery that makes everything that follows completely relevant and incredibly important.

Who am I?

It's a beginning that my author friend would be proud of.

If you have read any of my previous books, you can skip this chapter. You already know who I am and unless you need a quick refresher, you can skip straight to chapter 2. If not, then let me introduce myself.

My name is Anshul Raja. I am a British-Asian man who was born in Canada but grew up in London. My mother was a house wife; my dad an insurance broker. My parents adopted me when they were in their 40s, which meant there was always a significant age and cultural divide between us.

This placed me at somewhat of a disadvantage when it came to parental advice. In fact, everything I know about money and success came not from my parents, but from friends and other family members.

My biological dad and brother were also very inspiring and ambitious individuals, the sort who believe that anyone can achieve anything. That kind of mentality rubbed off on me from a very young age and has remained with me since.

Growing up, I assumed I would be rich and successful when I was older. I didn't know how I'd do it, but I knew I'd figure it out somehow. My career ambitions were almost completely influenced by TV or friends. After watching CSI, I decided I wanted to be a forensic scientist. ER led my aspirations down the surgical route, before the WWE transformed them into something equally bloody but much less caring.

Even though my career ambitions were all over the place, I knew that good grades would help me become successful later in life. At least, that's what everyone told me. I always tried my best in school, dreaming of one day scrutinising a crime scene or getting my hands on the WWE belt, but trying wasn't always good enough.

After receiving fairly average grades in my GCSEs and flopping my first year A-levels, I decided that enough was enough. The gap between who I was and who I wanted to be had grown too large and something inside me snapped. The sting of my bad grades combined with the motivation I received from older mentors drove me to improve my habits.

I developed a study strategy that helped me to turn three D grades and a U into straight As and I secured a place at my first-choice university. For the first time in my life, I stopped doubting myself and finally understood what 'believing in yourself' felt like!

At university, after a few hiccups during my first year, I used similar principles to achieve a first-class honours degree and an award for scoring one of the highest degree marks in my year group. It was at this point that I decided to share my story and methods with other struggling students, helping them to improve in the same way I had.

Initially, I mentored GCSE and & A-level students while working as a derivatives trader in the city. On one of the most difficult trading days of my career, I left the office and began writing a blog post on achieving good grades. What started as a random 1000-word blog turned into an entire book series ("How to ACE") designed to help 14-18 year olds succeed at school and college.

These books became number 1 best sellers in the Study Skills and Secondary Education categories on Amazon. Thousands of students have read and implemented my techniques.

Job Hunting

My academic results were on track by the time I reached my second year, but deciding on a career and finding an internship was much harder than I expected. It was more emotionally draining than I ever imagined. My first attempt at securing internships and work experience failed miserably.

During my first interview at an investment bank I was mumbling, fumbling, stuttering and giving terrible answers to basic questions. To make matters worse, the interviewer's colleague was a family friend so some people in my social circle learned about my humiliating failure. I failed largely because of my inefficient application strategy, but also due to my social skills.

Ignoring my mum's insistence that I was an incredibly smart and charismatic person, I took an objective look at my personality. What I found was not good at all, and it was a shame that I didn't become aware of this until university. My social skills—or lack thereof—should have been addressed much earlier in my life. Unfortunately, during parent-teacher discussions no one says, "You need to improve his emotional intelligence and ability to influence others or he'll struggle to get a job."

Thankfully, I took the necessary and sometimes extreme steps towards improving my charisma. *How to be Admired & Respected*, the second book in this series, describes the approach I took to turn myself from a mumbling, fumbling, socially anxious kid into a confident and influential young adult who interviewers said 'yes' to.

If you haven't already done so, you should read *How to be Admired & Respected* and begin the 6-month charisma project. Doing this will give you an edge over the other candidates you will be competing with. Securing a graduate job is more about understanding people than anything else.

The Strategy

Students tend to make the application process more complicated than it needs to be. For example, when applying to a Japanese bank, I read a 400-page book about the bank's history before attempting the application online. It was a massive waste of time as I didn't make it past the telephone interview. One of my friends banged out the application in half an hour, impressed in the assessment centre, and was offered an internship position.

After deciding what to apply for, I went though a process of trial and error to find the right strategy. I was constantly second guessing myself and I was desperate for someone to give me real direction instead of vague hints and tips.

That need for direction, that desperation for something substantial, was actually why I decided to write this book. It's everything I had wished for when I was that mumbling, fumbling, frustrated kid. It could have helped me then and I know it can help you now.

When I eventually found a rhythm, I received multiple offers from top investment banks and financial institutions, including a hedge fund in the middle east. I later completed a summer internship at one of the top investment banks in the world and became a full-time derivatives trader. I was the only person in my year to secure a decent summer internship/graduate job and a degree score above 70%.

At university, I became known as the 'go to' person when it came to graduate job applications and I loved helping my friends secure offers. People I barely knew requested my help with psychometric tests, applications and interviews. My approach was simple, but it worked!

Ever since university, I've mentored and served as a careers advisor to thousands of students like you.

Chapter 2
Who I Think you Are

Now I've told you who I am and what brought me here, what about you? Obviously, you can't tell me who you are, but you don't need to. I have a pretty good idea who you might be, where you are in your life and where you want to be.

You are most likely in one of three camps.

In the first camp are those who are just about to finish school/college and are preparing for an apprenticeship or for university. They're not particularly worried about their career right now and are more focused on Fresher's parties, new clothes, halls of residence, selfies, and how many "likes" their posts get. Finding and securing a good career isn't that high up on their 'to-do-list', just like it wasn't on mine. Most people in camp 1 believe they have already made their career decision.

"I am studying Chemical Engineering, therefore, I should be a Chemical Engineer"

When filling out my UCAS form, I assumed that I was choosing what I'd be doing for the rest of my life. I was wrong. After my degree, I learned that only 50% of UK graduates were working in a field relevant to their degree while 96% of degree holders had switched careers by the time they reached 24 years old.

If you are feeling anxious about exploring other options or changing your mind, don't be! I personally know dentist undergrads who are now investment bankers and engineers who are now medics.

Many undergrads and graduates don't change paths even when every bone in their body is telling them to because it seems like a large investment of effort and money. I get it. Spending two years studying another course or changing jobs may seem like a big chunk of your life. At 20 years old, 2 years is 10% of your life. Also, you probably only started thinking about your future at around 16, so 2 years is an eternity. However, in the context of your whole life, this is a tiny sacrifice. Ask any 30, 40 or 50 year old!

Even if you are hellbent on a career path, I encourage you to read this book with an open mind. The only way to truly know if a career path is right for you, is by trying it for several months. Reading about a job on a UCAS related website isn't enough.

If you are in camp 1, enjoy your first few months at university but make sure you know what's coming and prepare yourself by November latest. Here's the first of many golden nuggets in this book: ***Top companies tend to hire graduates through their internship programmes because they like to try before they buy.*** Many offer internships to first year university students and there are people just like you applying right now. This the trick to gaining work experience without having any 'proper' experience on your CV. Cue camp 2.

"How do I get a job when I have no work experience? How do I get work experience when I have nothing on my CV?"

This is by far the most common complaint I receive from those in camp 2 i.e. first and second year undergrads. Many of them thought they could focus on career stuff further down the line, but didn't realise how crucial work experience was. Yes, you can get a job without an internship, but it is so much harder! Why put yourself through that?

Of course, securing an internship depends on one very important factor: You need to know what career you want to go down. As you'll learn later in this book, picking a career is daunting for a number of reasons and choosing the best path takes time. Those who figure this out early are at a significant advantage because they can plan.

Camp 3 consists of those who are in their final year of university, as well as graduates. Your friends have already started applying, there is talk about CVs, interviews and assessment centres. At this point, you've probably realised how daunting and time-consuming job hunting is. It's almost as if you are doing a whole other degree.

It's even more difficult if you haven't decided what to do with your life and everyone around you seems to have it all figured out. Even if they don't admit it, almost everyone is second guessing themselves and they all fear making the wrong choice. This most certainly happened to me.

You don't need to have it completely figured out at this point. There are 30 year olds I know who are still second guessing themselves and sending messages in school group chats saying, 'has anyone really found their passion in life?'

Finding a fulfilling career is a long and iterative process. If you somehow pick the right career path for yourself on your first try, you'll be extremely lucky. Most people don't get it right the first time and have to jump around a little to find a reasonable fit. Finding the perfect fit—your *one true* passion in life— is a fallacy. It's like believing in the idea of a soulmate, whereby there is one perfect partner out there for everyone, even though everyone's perfect partner just so happens to live on the same street or go to the same university.

Your first 'real' job will be like your first boy/girlfriend. There will be elements that you intrinsically enjoy and ones you hate. Over time, you may come across another role that has more of those parts you enjoy. After a few boy/girlfriends, you will hopefully find one that is well suited to you and satisfies your needs.

At this stage, even if you've just narrowed your career choices down to a single industry, you're winning. Found a niche or specialisation that you are 60% sure of? You are miles ahead. Thousands of students in your position are in no man's land—their faces in the mud, their minds devoid of direction. If this is you, *How to Land Your Dream Graduate Job* will get you out of the trenches and on the right path.

Not knowing what to do next is normal. The majority of your peers are undecided at this stage, even if they don't admit it. Remember that you don't need to be 100% sure about what you want to do. You simply need a rough idea of the industry or type of job you want, based on a few factors that I'll show you later in this book. Having a rough idea will allow you to take an educated guess and find suitable career options.

This book is applicable for anyone between the ages of 16 and 25. Of course, out of the 10 million+ of you in this age group, my guidance will be relevant to some more than others.

Who this Book is Definitely for

Before beginning any monumental task, such as embarking on university or finding a career, I first pick out 3 relevant books online and/or ask older experienced people for advice. This is a habit I developed over time from realising that nothing, not even Google, can replace an experienced mentor or a well-structured resource written by someone who has achieved what I want to achieve. A decent book can give me 10 or so big golden nuggets, along with hundreds of smaller ones, that can save me mountains of time. If you're like me, this book is definitely for you and I hope it lands in your basket.

If you've never had a real full-time job before that paid you more than £1k per month, this book is also for you. Those who have taken gap years and sandwich years understand how much effort it takes to get a job offer. Most others underestimate this and pay the price later. That is why I usually recommend taking a gap year before starting university. Even if the job you do might be awful, the whole application and interview process will show you that none of this is complicated and will help you to develop your process. This is exactly what *How to Land Your Dream Graduate Job* will show you.

This book is also for those who are simply dragging their feet and avoiding making any choices. The freedom that university offers is a double-edged sword. On one side, it gives you autonomy; on the other it provides a lack of structure and zero accountability.

If you don't hand in your coursework or perform well in exams, you may receive warnings and there will be some social accountability too. However, if you go through university without securing an internship or work experience, no one is going to say anything to you. This isn't ideal, because building job skills and getting a good brand name on your CV can be just as valuable, if not more so, than some degrees.

This book is for those who understand there is a lot they don't know and see the value in receiving a heads-up from people a few years ahead of them. They are openminded enough to listen more than they talk, especially with someone who knows what they are talking about.

Reading it won't harm you and will benefit you. Worst-case scenario: it will plant a few important seeds that you can tend to later. Best case scenario: it will become your play-book for the next few years and ensure you land the perfect career.

Who this Book isn't for

Are you a 'flat earth' believer? If so, I doubt you'll find this book helpful. If you don't believe the evidence for the earth being an oblate spheroid then you probably aren't going to believe the evidence I put forward to you, some of which is from more 'open for interpretation' fields of study, such as social sciences.

This book isn't for cynical people who can't open their mind to new ideas. As a sceptical person myself, I understand how important it is to tell the difference between true and false. However, being so cynical that you discard every piece of advice given to you will stop you from growing as a person.

If you are in a specialised course such as medicine, dentistry, vet sciences or engineering, and you want to pursue those disciplines after university, then it's worth reading specialised books in addition to this one. I will help you tackle many important areas such as application strategy, developing a unique edge over other candidates and competency based interview questions. However, your employers will also ask specialised or technical questions to gauge your interest. This book will provide limited help with respect to these questions.

Chapter 3
What's in This Book

The first part of the book, 'First thing's first', will give you a brief history of our society and explain why you are on this path of birth-study-work-die. I'll spend a chapter defining what a good career looks like and then talk about alternative paths and human needs. Why do you crave a prestigious career, a high salary and letters after your name? Will any of it make you happy? You'll find out.

In the 'tangibles' section I'll discuss money. Most career books spend one chapter explaining why money doesn't matter and how you shouldn't make career decisions based on income. No one listens and the highest paying jobs continue to receive the highest number of applications each year. You can't build a capitalistic society then tell people not to care about money!

I agree that money shouldn't play a big part in your career decisions, but not for the reasons that are usually stated. Everyone knows that money doesn't buy happiness and no one needs to read a book to tell them that. But we also acknowledge that money can buy stability, security, food, health and holidays, things that can improve your happiness when you have them and destroy it when you don't.

Most people don't want money, they want the freedom that money awards them. For some this means being able to purchase what they want, but most just want to spend their time on anything they desire with few limitations. Money provides the freedom to spend time on activities that truly make people happy, like having a coffee with loved ones or committing to altruistic ventures. You don't need to be an investment banker to achieve this if you know what you're doing!

Instead of giving you a blanket statement like 'money doesn't buy you happiness', I am going to show you the relationship between money and happiness using academic evidence. Then, using a case study, I'll show you how people with middle-class salaries build large amounts of wealth over time and retire in their 40s. If money is important to you, by the end of this section you'll see how to become wealthy on a fairly average or slightly above average salary. However, the speed at which you create this wealth will be determined largely by what you are willing to sacrifice and by how many risks you are willing to take.

By the end of this chapter, I'll prove to you that you can achieve the freedom that you desire by picking a well-suited career then adopting the correct spending and investing habits rather than punting your time on ultra-high salary jobs.

Based on my argument, I'm hoping that you will do the right thing and choose a career based on your skillset *and* earning potential, not *just* your earning potential. I see this happen year on year and I can't ignore it anymore.

In the 'intangibles' section, I'll show you how true passion is rare and how it's more of a driver to push you forward rather than something you follow blindly. Identifying skills that you have developed over the past two decades of your life is a far better starting point to help you choose a career path. I'll then talk to you about identifying tasks that you intrinsically enjoy.

We'll use a 'self-stack' sheet to summarise all your key aptitudes on one A4 piece of paper. Spending some time fact-finding and putting together an honest representation of your skills will be one of the most valuable pieces of work you will do in your life. It may seem a little wishy-washy at first, but it's not. Trust me.

After running through intangibles with respect to your potential career paths, such as social status, stress and culture, I'll wrap this section up by defining what 'impact' in the workplace really means, and how applying your skills to a high-impact problem can provide a high-level of job satisfaction.

Having chosen a career path(s), in the second part of the book, I'll show you how to secure a job offer in the most efficient way possible using my PASC strategy.

P – Pick – Should I apply to small companies, large companies or both?

A – Aim – What type of job or companies should I apply to?

S – Shoot – What's the most efficient way to land an offer?

C – Check – What have I learnt about myself from this process?

I'll show you my 'reverse interview process', which goes into detail on building a winning CV and providing unique answers to competency questions. Then, finally, we'll cover streamlining hacks for your application process, interview preparation and how to achieve top psychometric test scores.

Everyone daydreams about their future and your career will play a big part in your life story. In the back of your mind you knew that this day was coming. Transitioning from education to the world of work does have its challenges but luckily there are habits you can proactively integrate into your day-to-day life that can give you a massive edge during the graduate job race. I'll provide you with a snapshot into your future that I wish someone had given me. By the end of this book you will know exactly how to approach the graduate job race and secure the career that you deserve.

First thing's first…

Chapter 4
Born-Study-Work-Die?

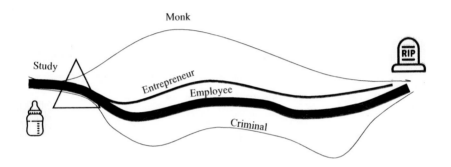

"Is this it? We're born, study, work then die?"

Every now and then someone asks me an existential crisis question like the above. You've asked yourself this question before, haven't you? Occasionally we look at our lives from a birds-eye view and ask ourselves, 'Is there another way? Is there a *better* way?'

We're all in the business of seeking fulfilment and reducing suffering. The decisions we make on a daily basis are designed to bring us closer to happiness. This is what humans do and it makes sense. If we're going to live our lives, why not 'optimise our fulfilment' in the most sustainable way possible?

Unfortunately, humans are notoriously bad at predicting what will deliver sustained satisfaction. Even when we do get an idea of what works, external influences and our internal biases stop us from acting in our own interests. This is why understanding 'gradualism' and forming good personal habits is important. Much of this book will focus on these things.

Ultimately, our time on this earth is finite and the choices we make every day determine what our overall fulfilment will be. Why not make informed choices based on evidence and reasoning rather than 'winging it'?

What Does the Evidence say?

"There was an elderly professor in my department who had been passionately keen on a particular theory for a number of years. One day an American visiting researcher came and he completely and utterly disproved our old man's hypothesis. The old man strode to the front, shook his hand and said, 'My dear fellow I wish to thank you. I have been wrong these 15 years'. We all clapped our hands raw! That was the scientific ideal of somebody who had a lot invested, a lifetime almost invested in the theory, and he was rejoicing that he had been shown wrong and that scientific truth had been advanced"
- *Richard Dawkins*

The majority of scientists choose their profession because they care about truth and finding correct answers to difficult questions, like 'how did life form on the earth?' and 'why is there something rather than nothing?'.

Scientists do everything to remove bias from their research and focus on empirical evidence. Some bad apples can be found amongst the bunch and these may fudge results. It's not a perfect system. However, most don't because they know someone in the scientific community will check their findings and expose them. This is essentially what the Peer Review system is. It allows the truth to bubble up to the surface, while the useless detritus remains on the bottom.

When I want answers to an important or difficult question, I begin with academic research. I look for publications that summarise academic findings and then I dig deeper into the sources that those authors used. Only then do I branch out and ask parents, friends and Google.

Scientists who find honest answers to difficult questions become heroes and celebrities in the scientific community. There are individuals you haven't heard of who are like the Kardashians of science. The difference is, they are judged on the integrity of their work and not how many likes they get on Instagram.

Psychological science will always be imperfect as it tries to observe someone else's subjective experience, but it's the best we've got and the closest we can get to understanding the inside of our minds. Despite the often 'wishy-washy' reputation of this area of science, when looking at hundreds or thousands of people, truths and patterns do start to emerge.

Having read over 80 publications, I'll give you an up to date summary of what the scientific community have to say about satisfaction in life and work. Then I'll share my interpretation on the research and use it to help you make good career decisions.

What Makes us Feel Fulfilled?

"Authentic happiness derives from raising the bar for yourself, not rating yourself against others."

Dr Martin Seligman is considered the 'father of positive psychology' and is one of the most cited psychologists ever. The quote above was taken from a chapter in his book, *Using the New Positive Psychology to Realise Your Potential for Lasting Fulfilment.* Seligman created a framework called PERMA to explore optimum human functioning and happiness.

Positive emotions – Experiencing more positive emotions than negative ones results in higher fulfilment levels. No surprise there! About a third of us are genetically predisposed to see the glass half-full rather than half-empty. Cheerfulness can be inherited.

Engagement – Have you ever been so absorbed in a task that you lost track of time? That's what some scientists call 'flow'. Experiencing this phenomenon regularly improves life and job satisfaction. We'll talk more about this in the next chapter.

Relationships – We need, neurologically, to know that we belong to a group. It helps us feel safe and valued, and it has done for millions of years. One of the longest studies on happiness, which tracked the development of 724 people over 75 years, showed that good relationships keep us happier and healthier.

Meaning – Psychological studies correlate meaning in life to life satisfaction, well-being, optimism, response to stress, and happiness. *Meaning* comes in three flavours. The first type of meaning is *Sense-making*. This is where we understand how the world works. We declare to ourself: "I understand the meaning of this…" The second type of meaning, *Purpose*, is where we experience life by setting goals. We may think or say, "The meaning of my life is to …" *Worth* is the third type of meaning and is where we assess the value or significance of our life. "My life has meaning because …"

When you assess your life for its meaning, you are measuring yourself against your personally assigned criteria for one or more of these factors. You are measuring yourself against this question, or one similar: *How much meaning does my life have?*

Accomplishment – In all research related to well-being, stagnation and passiveness are the enemies of happiness. As humans we have to keep progressing and need intellectual stimulation. Achieving this is very difficult if we don't know where we're going, and that's why setting goals and working towards them is critical for fulfilment.

We'll use Seligman's model to help us decide what job characteristics we should prioritise when choosing a career path. Another way to answer this question is by looking at human needs.

What do we Need?

When people discuss human needs, they usually bring out a framework. Nine times out of ten this is Maslow's Hierarchy of Needs. Maslow's work was published in the mid 1900s and is still used to describe how our needs influence our motivations. It can be a useful model to help us understand fulfilment too:

Existence

1. *Physiological:* Oxygen, food, and water. These are the things necessary to maintain life and they are required by all animals.

2. *Safety:* When an individual's physiological needs are met, the focus shifts to safety needs, which may include health and financial security.

Relatedness

3. *Community and belonging:* If safety and physiological needs are met, a person will focus on the need for a community and love. Friends, family, and romantic partners usually fulfil this need.

4. ***Esteem:*** This is necessary for self-actualisation. A person may work to achieve esteem once needs for love and a sense of belonging are met. Self-confidence and acceptance are important components of this need.

Growth

5. ***Self-actualisation:*** This is the ability to meet one's true potential, and the necessary components of self-actualisation vary from person to person. A writer may be self-actualised when able to complete a series of top selling novels, for instance.

6. ***Self-transcendence:*** This involves the expansion of personal boundaries, including experiencing spiritual ideas such as considering oneself as an integral part of the universe.

Maslow stated that once we have our basic physical and safety needs sorted, we feel more ready to share ourselves with others and accomplish things in the world. Most people can readily identify with these common levels of motivation.

Maslow held that as we come to feel satisfied with our accomplishments and sense of social worth, we take another step. He referred to this urge as **self-actualisation**. It is very similar to the process Carl Jung referred to as **individuation**, which tends to kick-in during mature adulthood.

Self-actualisation is different from all the previous needs. We don't feel spurred into action by a sense of *deficiency* ("Must find food…" "Must make friends…"). Rather, we feel inspired to *grow*, to explore our potential and become more of what we feel we can be. Maslow called self-actualisation a growth need while all the rest are deficiency needs.

Maslow later spoke about an additional level in the pyramid called 'transcendence'. This is when someone moves beyond self-actualisation and puts their needs aside, to a great extent, in favour of service to others. At this level, there is a desire is to go beyond our ordinary human level of consciousness and experience oneness with the greater whole, the higher truth, whatever that may be.

Academics still contest Maslow's theories but their widespread use proves that it's an excellent explanation of human nature. Whenever I explain this to someone for the first time, their reaction says it all. They immediately recognise this model in themselves and in others around them.

Maslow's theory originally suggested that one level of the hierarchy must be satisfied in order to progress to the next— you don't care about fulfilling creative tasks if you don't have enough money to buy food. In reality, and what most psychologists agree on, many different motivations from various levels of Maslow's hierarchy can occur at the same time.

This means that at any given moment your decisions can be governed by physiological, safety, love & belonging, esteem and self-actualisation all at the same time. However, there is often one dominant need that is at play depending on your stage of self-development.

If your physiological needs have been met, which is true for most people in developed nations, there will be a tipping point where your need for love/belonging will become stronger than your need for safety. Your need for the basics in life will be there, but they won't cause you tension and anxiety.

Why is understanding our needs important? It's not so much the needs themselves, but the gap between your needs and you. Or the gap between you and who you want to be. The key to living a fulfilling life is ensuring the gap between the two doesn't grow too large.

Preventing Catastrophe

"Fulfilment is dependent on the gap between you and your needs"
  - Anshul Raja

The smaller the gap between your expectations and reality, the more fulfilled you will feel. For example, if you needed to pass university and completed 2nd year with an average score of 68%, your life satisfaction rating would be positively affected.

On the contrary, a large gap between your reality and needs will create more negative emotions than positive. For example, if you expected to be on a well-respected career path by age 21 and have no interviews lined up in your final year of university, your life satisfaction rating will probably be lower than average. This can be dangerous if left untreated.

If the gap stays large for too long or keeps growing larger, your mind can snap. Some mental health issues can develop, including post-traumatic stress disorder, anxiety, depression, and emotional experiences such as fear, anger, shame, and sadness.

Transitioning between the education and career phase can be very difficult for some people. This is when a 'quarter-life crisis' can occur and is caused by the expectations built-up from two decades of adolescence colliding with the reality of adulthood. Many beliefs you have concerning relationships, money, fulfilment and health will be tested in your 20s. As your belief systems toss and turn, so will you!

The National Survey of Drug Use and Health states, 'The prevalence of adults with a major depressive episode is highest among individuals between 18 and 25.' The Office of National Statistics in the UK states, 'Young people aged 16–24 were more likely to report suicidal thoughts than any other age group'. Almost half of my closest friends experienced some form of depression or anxiety within the first 2 years of graduation. Two of them unfortunately never recovered.

There are two ways you can prevent this from happening and feel more fulfilled: you can either dampen your needs or enhance your reality. People tend to lean towards the latter and invest their time into maintaining and enhancing their reality to meet their needs.

Enhancing your Reality

People go to university, find jobs and buy books like this to meet their career needs. They go to the gym and go on multiple dates to meet their relationship needs. We all tend to do this this because we feel that meeting these needs will result in a more satisfying life.

Many people imply that working your way up Maslow's hierarchy or using it as a framework will bring you happiness. This is not what Maslow claimed and it's only partially true.

If your physiological needs aren't met, you're not going to experience happiness. That's pretty obvious. However, fulfilling social and growth needs will feel like you're chasing your own tail. The goalposts keep moving and your needs will keep running away from you.

Most 30-40 year olds I speak to explain how their expectations are always miles away from their reality no matter what they do. At 16, they thought getting good grades and going to university would bring them more happiness and it did, to an extent. At 18, they thought getting a top job with good pay would make them happier and at 25 it became all about promotions and a long-term partner. These things brought them happiness, but only for a short while and never to the extent they expected. And so the cycle continues.

We are biologically programmed to want more resources and command more respect from our peers and this is true no matter how much of those things we have.

I think everybody should get rich and famous and do everything they ever dreamed of so they can see that it's not the answer.

- Jim Carey

Our genes are somewhat selfish because don't care about our fulfilment. They care about survival and procreation, that's it. This part of our DNA code is the reason every living creature exists right now. This focus trickles into our psyche and causes us to want more than we have—more sexual partners, promotions, prestige, accomplishments, assets, praise and money. If we focus entirely on our needs, there will always be a gap between who we are and who we want to be.

You could say that we have biologically evolved to never be fully satisfied.

Given that we all know this happens, why don't we focus on getting rid of our needs instead? Can we fight biology? Is there any point? In a perfect utopian society there might be a chip we could implant in our brains to eradicate desires of money, relationships and material possessions. Doing so would make everyone much happier, but also bring the human race to a halt.

How to Make our Needs Meet us

It is possible to dampen our needs, but it's not easy. This is mainly because of the evolutionary reasons I mentioned earlier, but also because we don't consciously choose our needs, they choose us. Removing them requires hours of intense introspection and, in most cases, a complete removal of oneself from modern society.

Imagine that I place a button in front of you and explain that if pressed, this button will eliminate 99% of your desires and needs. Friends, romantic relationships, family, academic results, employment, money, nice clothes—all those desires would disappear. Would you push it?

Most of us wouldn't as it's scary notion. Imagine not needing your own mum? Yet, people do choose to press this button and the results are remarkable.

I personally know two people who have done this. Both were men who left high flying careers in Canada and Australia to join a monastery near Los Angeles. They spend most of their time practicing various forms of introspection, usually meditation, to dampen their needs and achieve self-transcendence. Both of them love being there and plan to spend the rest of their days there.

For the rest of us, living in modern society with our families and friends, our needs aren't going anywhere. Some of these needs will be met today and some wont. This doesn't mean we will be miserable forever. We are all capable of living fulfilling lives in modern society by investing our time into meeting our most basic needs. However, a little introspection from time to time is important.

Everyone admires the wealthy western countries for what they've achieved, but when it comes to being truly fulfilled at work and living fulfilled lives, we can learn from the east.

Monks do not feel anxiety, depression or have mental health issues. Studies on their brains have revealed different patterns when compared to the brains of people living a stressful, demanding existence. Monks spend a long time practicing various methods, like meditation, that focus on appreciating the here and now. Some spend hours doing this every day and, over time, this changes the brain. One study conducted on monks and nuns, by the University of Bristol, showed that those who had been meditating for a number of years were less susceptible to psychological distress than those practicing for shorter periods of time.

Meditation is a fulfilment hack. If you focus on the present moment and on being grateful for what you currently have rather than what you don't have, eventually you won't feel the need to desire more than you already have. The more hours you spend thinking in this way, the more fulfilled you will feel.

In my opinion, fulfilment requires a combination of meeting and dampening needs simultaneously. This means building the right habits to fulfil most of our human needs and using various techniques every day to dampen them.

I've spent the last few years practicing what I now preach. I spend long hours enhancing my reality, writing books, growing my business, etc., I also spend many hours a week using techniques to focus on the present moment and remind myself of what I have. This is usually accomplished through various forms of meditation, but not always. My partner and I deliberately talk about what we are grateful for every week. Doing so for the last few years has kept my life satisfaction rating at an average of 8.

Usually, when I talk about meditation to university undergrads, I see a lot of eye-rolls and hear a lot of sighs. They are firmly focused on getting a degree and getting a job and don't really want to hear about fulfilment. I get that—it makes sense.

However, I want to plant this seed early because you're going to need it later.

Here are some gems from Mr Maslow himself:

"Happiness may actually be a by-product, an epiphenomenon, of something that comes en passant. The best way to realize retrospectively that you were happy, even though you lacked awareness at the time, is to be committed to a worthy task or cause and to work in a dedicated way for it."
-   (Maslow, 1996, pp. 23-24)

"Happiness will have to be defined as being pained & troubled in a good cause! The good life is to have good-real-worthwhile worries & anxieties."
-   (Maslow, 1979, p. 403)

Highly evolved individuals assimilate their work into the identity, into the self—work actually becomes part of the self, part of the individual's definition of himself. Work can be psychotherapeutic, psychogogic (making well people grow toward self-actualisation).

Maslow believed that finding the *right* work for yourself meant you could toil joyfully and endlessly at the task because, "you've found your path". This is what he told an audience in 1969 just months before he died. Doing the work that's right for you, even with a normal life "expectancy of about 70 or 75 years or so, it could be *175 years* and that would be endless."

Doing the right work, in other words, enhances life, Maslow believed. It helps one to flourish.

A Brief History of Society and your Role in it

We were all born without direction and plonked on a path we didn't choose. Our minds were shaped by others and we've been led to believe that if we work hard enough, we'll get what we want in life and will be happy. They weren't lying, but they didn't exactly tell us the whole truth. These are words that I would never have dreamt of saying as a rebellious contrarian 20-year-old who took big risks after graduating.

Despite what the media says, western democratic governments are designed to keep the masses content. Years of seesawing between political parties and 'the people' has created multiple social, economic and legal systems built to fulfil our needs.

For example, in most developed nations, the first two levels of Maslow's hierarchy are satisfied. 99.5% of those in the UK have continuous access to shelter, food and water. We have financial benefits and free healthcare—our peers won't let us starve if we can't buy food, they won't let us freeze if we can't pay rent and they won't let us die if we're ill.

87% of people in the UK say they feel safe walking alone after dark. We all collectively pay for Police and Fire services and crime rates are low when compared to many other countries.

Government and economic systems are in place to ensure our

physical needs are also taken care of even when we're too old to support ourselves. We pay into 'National Insurance' and state pension schemes when we're young so that we can receive a steady stream of money when we're old.

Married people receive certain tax benefits because they are, statistically speaking, the kind of people most governments want. They are more likely to settle down and assimilate into a community, which is good for social cohesion. They are more likely to buy houses and to feed into the economy with major purchases, which boosts the government coffers. They are also more likely to have children and raise them in a stable environment, thus contributing to population growth.

These children are provided with access to mandatory schooling until the age of 16, with free or subsidised secondary education thereafter to ensure they grow into educated, constructive members of society.

All these man-made systems are intricately connected to ensure model citizens have their basic needs covered and are provided with the means they need to live comfortably. It also ensures these citizens are provided with the tools they need to grow, to progress and to thrive, after which they can get a job, make money and feed back into the system.

As a university student, apprentice or graduate employee you are a model citizen. By the time you reach the age of 20, society will have invested significant resources into your upbringing and they will probably achieve a decent return, both tangible and intangible, on that investment. According to Walter W McMahon from the University of Illinois, you will return more than £8,500 per year in social <u>non-market</u> benefits to society.

So, what's in it for you?

You now have most of what you need to fulfil your human needs and to live a satisfying life. Not only are your physical needs covered, but you have a great opportunity to fulfil your social and growth needs too.

According to the 'Understanding Society UK Household Longitudinal Study', 79.7% of people were either somewhat or completely satisfied with their jobs. 30% of the sample stated that their overall life satisfaction rating was 9 or 10 out of 10. When candidates were asked how worthwhile they felt the things they do were, 36% said 'very worthwhile'.

Gallup polls show the average life satisfaction rating of western countries is around 7/10. Which is not bad compared to poorer nations where ratings are 5 or less.

7 is your baseline. Day to day and week to week your life satisfaction rating may fluctuate. However, across months and

years you will probably be pretty content. The media will occasionally make you feel that other people are happier than you because they are rich and famous, but this isn't true. If you look back on your last 6 months and feel you are less than a 7/10, you have an unsatisfied need that needs to be resolved. Make no mistake, you and *only you* are responsible for your own happiness.

The aforementioned welfare systems do a good job of keeping us fulfilled relative to the rest of the world. You may not be happy today or tomorrow, but by being a model citizen who plays by the rules—achieves educational qualifications, gets a job, finds a life partner—you have a high chance of being satisfied with your life in the long-term.

This is why most people choose to be model citizens instead of vagabonds or criminals. This is why we're constantly being told to take the path most trodden and be as much of a model citizen as we can be. The system works and everyone knows it works, so they advise accordingly.

Of course, we could still screw it up. It's ultimately our responsibility to develop the right habits and to ensure our life satisfaction remains at 7 or above.

Born-Study-Work-Die?

Sustained lasting fulfilment is all that really matters so it's all we should be aiming for. Forget about prestige or popularity— stop daydreaming about superstardom and incalculable riches. If you keep coming back to this truth and base your decisions around it, you'll look back on your life fondly and won't be filled with regret.

The systems all around us work well. By simply being born into a wealthy country and following the path we've been told to follow, most of our needs have already been taken care of. You now have the opportunity to carve out a fulfilling life, and your career plays a significant role in doing so.

Even if you narrow your career options down to six reasonable options and roll the dice, you're more likely to land on a ful- filling path than an unfulfilling one. Of course, we don't want to leave it all to chance. Finding a compatible career, like find- ing a compatible life partner, is a gamble. There is no proven formula and there definitely isn't a "soulmate" just waiting around the corner. It's a series of best practices based on scien- tific evidence and collective wisdom.

We have a good chance of finding work that has a positive im- pact on our overall life, but it isn't a guarantee. 21.3% of those surveyed in the Understanding Society UK Household Longitudinal Study said they were not satisfied with their work. And of the 79.7% who felt positively about their jobs, only 17.2% said they were completely satisfied.

One of the objectives of this book and the Level Up series is to ensure you end up on the right side of this statistic.

Chapter 5
What Does a Good Job Look Like?

Growing up, my idea of a good career was largely influenced by what I saw on TV. I wanted to be a forensic scientist, a doctor—whatever program I was obsessed with at that moment became my career of choice. Being an adult with a cool job seemed way more exciting than being at school.

'A good career is one that's thrilling.'

I learnt how satisfying it was to earn my own money when I got my first paper round. It gave me a sense of responsibility and freedom I had never felt before. I realised that a job was a simple transaction: my time for their money. The more experience I acquire, the more money they'll give me; the more money I make, the more freedom I'll enjoy.

'A good career is one that's thrilling and pays well.'

Before applying to university, I saw my future career as way to enhance my social status. To have a degree and be a professional was a prestigious achievement and, if I were to succeed,

What Does a Good Job Look Like?

I would be somewhere towards the top of the social hierarchy. People would respect me and everyone wants to be respected.

'A good career is one that I'm passionate about, is thrilling, pays well and improves my social value.'

My career decisions at university were based on the above definition and I only chose jobs that ticked all these boxes. During my internship, I realised that many of these assumptions were incomplete. Yes, a job can be exciting. I could be the hero, make an impact and high-five my colleagues. But it wouldn't always be like that.

At times, my work consisted of mundane tasks like dealing with invoices, paperwork and excel sheets. It also came with a lot of anxiety and stress—performance anxiety, office politics, high-pressure situations.

I realised prestige was highly overrated. Being greeted by the security guard as I walked through the glass doors in a new suit made me feel important. For about a week. Sure, I loved seeing people react when I told them where I worked, but by the end of the internship none of that prestige mattered.

'A good career is one that is thrilling, pays well, is interesting and doesn't stress me out.'

My definition of a good career moulded itself over many years as a result of my experiences. Eventually, I arrived at a definition that agreed with academic evidence and manoeuvred myself into a job that I loved. Having tracked my life satisfaction over the years, it has never been higher than it is now, and this has a lot to do with my career choices.

From interviewing hundreds of students, we found that most people ignore the evidence, especially those who have strong beliefs about themselves or the career they feel suited to. Unfortunately, these beliefs are often plagued with bias.

Chapter 6

Should you Follow your Passion?

I woke up with a hangover, my brain apparently trying to beat a path out of my skull as my stomach lurched this way and that, like a seasick sailor trying to ride out a storm. I was staying in a £2m villa located on a palm-shaped island in Dubai, but all the sunshine and opulence in the world won't cure a hangover borne of too many vodka-shots and too little sleep.

A I walked down the stairs, the smell of perfume invaded my nostrils and turned my stomach. It was a new scent, but the experience was all-too familiar. Over the course of the previous 3 weeks I had encountered numerous different fragrances wafting through the expansive corridors. I could almost see the thick scent flume as it marked a path from my brother's bedroom, across the hallway, down the stairs and out the door. It was the villa's own "walk of shame".

My suspicions were confirmed when I heard the front door shut. I went straight to my brother's room to catch up on the night before. As I walked in, he was on his desk clicking away in front of 6 LCD screens covered in charts. He looked like a fighter pilot. Sitting next to him, I saw his 'profit & loss' figure that showed how much money he had made so far that day. It said +$239,999. It was such a memorable moment for me that I still remember the number.

There were several others living in the villa too. One was a lawyer, another a consultant and a guy called Jay who worked for an Indian billionaire. Jay started his career at an investment bank and then was headhunted to manage a £100 million fund for a tycoon.

While my friends at home spoke about football and moaned about their lecturers at uni, these guys spoke about building tech start-ups and buying Ferraris. While my mates at home danced in a circle in a pub occasionally trying to talk to passing girls, these guys had a table waiting for them in the club with girls hovering around. I'd never met anyone like them before. I mean, I'd seen this stuff in movies and music videos but I never really thought people lived like this until I saw it for myself. At 19 years old, this had an enormous influence on me.

I was heartbroken the day I had to leave the villa, crying my eyes out in the taxi to the airport. However, the moment I sat down on the flight, I began brainstorming and mapping out various plans for the future. I'd never felt so inspired and I couldn't wait to get started on my own journey to success.

Should you Follow your Passion?

Passion

In the weeks that followed, I ran around like a headless chicken trying to figure out what to do next. My end goal was to live a life of freedom, surrounded by like-minded people and with few limitations. How was I going to do it?

At the time, my answer was to get into a position where I managed mine and other people's money. I couldn't get the memories of Dubai out of my head—my brother in front of all those screens and the +$239,999, as well as the freedom, girls, and fun that went along with it.

My brother and his friends introduced me to new pathways that I never considered before—finance, investment banking, law, wealth management, algorithmic trading and entrepreneurship. I thought that if they had achieved their success via those pathways, then I could achieve the same. I was impressionable, as most 19 year olds are, and my reasons for pursuing this career path were shallow and misguided.

Before leaving Dubai, my brother and Jay recommended that I open a simulator trading account to help me learn. They also gave me a reading list which I finished a week after coming back to the UK. I became obsessively interested in how professional money managers predicted price movements in markets.

To me, the capital markets was one big game that hundreds of thousands of people around the world played every day. As a trader, I could become one of the best players in the world and build an incredible life for myself. It all made sense!

Everyone had told me that it was important to "follow your passion", but how was I to know what was a passion and what was a passing fad? I asked myself this question for weeks and bothered all of my friends with it as well.

This fantasy of my future life was the 'ring' and I was Frodo, doing everything I could to get there. I made a bunch of assumptions about what I needed to do to succeed. I was convinced that I first needed my degree (70%+) or I wouldn't stand a chance against the Oxbridge candidates I was up against. This wasn't accurate! I also assumed that I needed to proactively improve my charisma and ability to influence others to win over interviewers. This was spot on!

Despite some wrong assumptions, my efforts paid off and I secured several offers from some of the best companies in the industry. Eventually I landed a graduate position at a prop trading firm which was more or less where I wanted to be.

My final year of university was one the most productive periods of my life. All the steps I took removed the social anxiety I'd been carrying since school, got me a first-class honours degree, an academic award, a great brand name on my CV, graduate job and ultimately the content for this book. For a long time, I assumed my intense passion caused this uptick in performance, until I met my old friend Vincent.

Parallel Universe

Vincent was a smart and ambitious guy who also happened to have a similar vision to me while at university. I met him in the investment society at UCL. He was equally, if not more pas-sionate about becoming a trader in the financial markets. We spoke and exchanged ideas a number of times during second year. He had also been trading foreign exchange markets using his student loan since first year with good results.

When I came back to uni after the summer, I discovered that he dropped out of his course and moved back home. We lost touch. Several years later, he sent me a message on LinkedIn asking if I wanted to catch up and I agreed.

This is when I learned what had happened to Vincent. It was a discovery that changed my own trajectory.

After underperforming in his second-year exams, Vincent de-cided to 'follow his passion' and trade full time from home. He created a fund for himself by combining what was left of his student loan with some money from his parents. He went through a cycle of making and losing money for several years until his parents held an intervention, pulled the plug and sent him to a psychotherapist.

"I basically need to get a job—if only I stayed at uni!"

This was one of the last comments he made to me before we parted ways and it got me thinking:

Don't follow your passion blindly

Being passionate about an idea or vision for yourself is a powerful driver. It will get you out of the bed each morning, but won't tell you what to do with your day. You still need to do your due diligence, listen to advice from specialists, be strategic and make rational choices. Intense passion only turns up the heat under the pan. You still need to add the right ingredients.

Both Vincent and I were deeply passionate about the same vision. How did we end up miles apart? We both ultimately fell short of our multi-million pound targets, but I had a top degree from a top university and a strong brand name on my CV, all of which I leveraged to build Academic Underdogs and the book you are reading today.

It's not that I didn't think about leaving university and getting started on my own. I actually considered that a lot. I knew that trading had a low probability of success. If I did succeed, brilliant, but what if I failed? What if I failed to hit my £650k target in 4 years? Surely having a degree and some solid work experience would give me a safety net. I could leverage my qualifications and experience to get a job or start another business. That option would exist for me. This isn't about being timid, it's about being smart and covering your downside. It's about manoeuvring yourself into a win-win situation or as close to it as possible.

Should you Follow your Passion?

Can you relate to my story? Do you have a vision for the future and yourself? Do you fantasise about that vision and how to get there? Do you read, listen or watch content around this area of interest? Has this feeling been around for more than a month and withstood criticism from people close to you? If so, congratulations, you are probably in love with your future self.

Passion is an intangible metric similar to love. As a data-driven, evidence-based person, I sometimes have an issue getting my head around these emotions. When my other half asks me how much I love her, I stretch my arms out wide and say 'this much', but in my head, I'm thinking 'how long is a piece of string?'.

Over time, I've become much less sceptical and appreciate how powerful these psychological quirks can be, especially when breaking through personal plateaus and achieving success. I attribute much of my progress at university to the emotional state that I was in, but as you'll soon find out, passion can also negatively affect your decision making.

Use your vision to push you forward, but don't use it as an excuse to make uninformed decisions. You still need to learn about yourself, gather data about various career paths and strategically move forward.

Our minds are incredibly good at complex tasks and problem solving, but we are terrible at figuring out what makes us happy in the future. Recency bias is a psychological effect that prioritises recent experiences over older ones. An argument with someone after a great night out shouldn't influence your feelings of the overall evening, but unfortunately it does. This happens somewhat unconsciously and its effect can negatively affect your ability to distinguish between a good and bad career.

Home bias is another one. Relatives have a strong influence on your perception of what a good career looks like and ultimately your career decisions. One study by Facebook data scientists, which analysed over 5.6 million parent-child and 2.7 million sibling pairs, showed 'that people within a family are proportionally more likely choose the same occupation.'

Your relatives know you better than anyone else and mean well, but their advice isn't always best. They might also be passing their biases onto you. Beginning with principles and then letting evidence guide your decisions would be a more prudent approach.

There is several decades worth of research available on happiness, life and work satisfaction. Yet most people, including myself, never bothered to cross check their beliefs with evidence or read books that summarise the evidence. It's your lucky day!

Chapter 7
What Should I Aim for in a Career?

Only after working in a job for a few years, did I look at the evidence and act on it. Moving from financial markets to running my education business helped me define my final definition of a good career.

'A good career is engaging, meaningful and one that I'm good at'

Engagement

'What makes a job satisfying?' Many scientists from different fields have tried answering this question. Oldham, Hackman, Cross, Locke, Khaleque and Rahma are some of the heroes that came up with answers that stuck. Scientists don't agree all that often, however, in this particular scenario, many researchers agree on the characteristics that create job satisfaction.

The Job Characteristic Model (JCB) was developed by hero scientists Oldham and Hackman. It suggested that people were satisfied with their jobs when the work was engaging. Nothing groundbreaking! They then defined exactly what engaging work consisted of using these five components:

1. ***Task identity*** – Having an obvious beginning and end

An orthopaedic surgeon's job involves doing a whole and iden-tifiable piece of work. If a patient comes into the surgery with a broken leg, the surgeon fixes it and her job is pretty much done.

In contrast, the beginning and end of a psychotherapist's work is less obvious. People with severe mental health issues don't always recover and the job is more about management than cure.

2. ***Autonomy*** – To what extent does your job permit you to decide how to go about doing the work?

Engagement increases when you have the freedom to reach your end goal in whichever way you see fit. Without a sense of choice in how or why we approach a task, we will begin to lose interest.

3. ***Skill & task variety*** – How many different types of tasks do you do?

Variety is the enemy of boredom. Unfortunately, the modern job market forces us to specialise because it's more productive.

In the Pre-1900s, people didn't specialise and often conducted many tasks every day. There were around 200 different professions back then and now there are over 5000! This is called the division of labour.

4.   *Task significance* – Do you think your work is significant or meaningful?

Meaningfulness or significance occurs when we feel we're contributing to something bigger than ourselves; which could be a team, company or wider society. People who consider their jobs to be meaningful are happier, healthier, and more reliable.

5.   *Feedback* – Does the work itself tell you when the job's done?

The surgeon knows that, when the patient is sewn up and the heart rate monitor is beeping away, she's done a good job. Continuous feedback from the job itself or from others increases engagement.

Have you ever played a strategy game like Rise of Nations or Sid Meier's Civilisation? When playing these games, your goal is to build a civilisation and defeat other opponents. You start with one person or unit and the game ends when all but one opponent is killed. There is a clearly identified start and finish; you have *task identity*. No one tells you how to win. You can build up your base and defence and then attack, or you can go all-guns blazing early—you have complete *autonomy*. There are thousands of moves, decisions and combinations you can make; you have *variety*. If you are attacked, buildings and vehicles/infantry can be weakened or destroyed. When attacking units beat opponents in battle, they gain experience and strength. Scoring displays show all these metrics and provide regular *feedback*.

Games, and in particularly strategy games, are the most engaging devices man has ever made. Nothing holds our attention better. When playing these games as a kid, my engagement level was so high that I would sometimes forget to eat for the whole day.

A career is quite simply a set of tasks that you do over a prolonged period of time. If these tasks share the same characteristics that a strategy game has, you will reach a state of flow regularly.

Flow

After a summer internship at a big bank, I finally got what I wanted and joined a proprietary trading firm in London. This firm was labelled as a place for 'investment banking rejects' but I didn't care. Having done my research, there were several successful traders there who were pulling in north of £500k a year. If they can do it, I thought, then I can too. They didn't pay a salary, but the commission structure seemed good and it seemed like a good place to start.

Manual or 'point and click' trading was very similar to playing a video game. I had full *autonomy* and no two days were the same, so plenty of *variety*. Each trade had an open and close. Each trading day started and ended at exactly the same time too. My job was to make money and end the day 'green', a very clear *task identity*. Every day was made up of smaller trades, and the outcome of these trades provided regular *feedback*.

It didn't take long for me to move from the simulator to the 'live market'. This is when the company gave me real money to trade. Any profits I made were split between me and the firm, and losses were absorbed by the company. It looked like a great deal! I had some financial backing, a good environment to learn and all the tools I needed to be successful. The rest was down to me.

Over the next year, I had several good runs followed by bad runs. I ended the year 'flat'. Making enough to cover my expenses but a fraction of the amount my friends made in salaried work. It wasn't great but I was convinced that the more I practiced the better I'd get.

A year later I had made very little progress and I began to wonder if I had failed. Mentors at the company repeated again and again "never give up on your dreams" and "it takes 10,000 hours to become good at something". Instead of quitting, I stepped up my game.

What Should I Aim for in a Career?

During most days, particularly when the market was moving around, I would be in a constant state of flow. However, when the market was slow or after a trading day, I felt miserable. There were two possible reasons for this:

1.   I was not good at my job
2.   My life and career lacked meaning

Be Good at What you do

My lack of results as a 'point and click' trader had nothing to do with hard work. I read every book under the sun, spoke to hundreds of successful traders and was praised for being the first in and last out every day.

Unfortunately, my skills and psychological make up didn't lend itself to the job. Even though my performance, in relation to others, was average, instinctively I knew that my rate of progress was far too slow and was negatively impacting my happiness. Those days were very dark and it felt like I had a dark cloud following me around. Everyone close to me knew this too.

As Maslow's and Dr Seligman's model suggest, accomplishment is a human need and a key component of fulfilment. We all need to see growth in our lives and stagnation is not only painful, but dangerous to our mental health.

My initial choice to become a trader wasn't wrong. I'd always had an affinity towards numbers more than words, and a genuine interest in the financial markets. There were elements of 'point and click' trading that I was good at, like generating profitable trade ideas and understanding economic announcements. However, my emotions and the way in which I responded to losing money let me down.

Looking back there were some clues in my childhood that may have suggested this weakness, but as Mr Jobs said, it's much easier to connect the dots looking backwards than forwards. I needed to try the job first to see if I had what it took. Unfortunately, I didn't, so I pivoted towards a different style of trading called 'evidence based trading'.

Instead of making the trading decisions myself, I learnt how to programme algorithms to trade for me. This style of trading was much more suited to my personality and prevented my emotions from interfering with the trading process. Thankfully the first algorithm I built worked and my performance improved, along with my job satisfaction. Unfortunately, it wasn't long before I found myself in the doldrums again. There was another key ingredient missing from my work and life: *meaning*.

Meaning

Performing better and making more money didn't satisfy me for long. At this point, I felt like my standards were probably

63

too high. People told me to stop being a typical moaning millennial and that no job is perfect. I didn't listen and started to take action.

Upon reading about meaning, I noticed this word appeared everywhere across positive psychology and life satisfaction literature. It had appeared in both Seligman and Oldham & Blackmans publications. Yet the definition of the term is quite unclear and there is no objective standard to measure it.

This frustrated me until I realised that when it comes to meaning, we create our own definition. It's the story we tell ourselves every day as to why we are doing what we are doing. It could be *'I am doing this to improve my family's life'* or *'I am working towards this because we may be the only intelligent life in the universe and we need to become a space-faring civilisation'*. In case you didn't notice, the last one was from Elon Musk.

So, what is meaning? In asking a question like this, *you* have set the standard, *you* have set the measure, and *you* are doing the testing! Meaning is whatever you personally care about and only you can answer this question. As a rule of thumb, in the attempt to find meaningful career, you can't go wrong with choosing one that helps other people.

Almost every strand of philosophy states in some way that fulfilment is closely related to altruism. Studies—even the less wishy-washy ones—done with brain scans show that altruistic behaviour increases serotonin levels in the brain. People on their deathbed never say 'I regret spending all those hours helping others'.

In an attempt to inject more meaning into my life, I started mentoring students that were struggling to improve their grades. Hearing the woes of underperforming capable students always struck a nerve with me because I used to be one of them.

After receiving my poor first year A-level grades, my data was placed into an algorithm to help me and the school determine what my future targets should be. It suggested that I had a small chance of achieving straight As. These algorithms aren't always right but they are capable of making good predictions within a small margin of error. There were always anomalous students that defied the odds, and I happened to be one of them!

Receiving lower than expected grades created an emotional wound, but overcoming the doubt and fear and becoming an award-winning student created a meaningful memory, one that has stayed with me and constantly reminds me, 'I've been the anomaly once and I can be it again'.

This is why I chose to mentor students rather than volunteer at a homeless shelter. I'm sure someone who has been homeless before would find the latter more meaningful. Looking at events in your past, triumph or trauma or both, can help determine what you care about. Knowledge of this can help you find a meaningful career.

What Should I Aim for in a Career?

Unsurprisingly, I absolutely loved helping students improve and was damn good at it too. What started with my mum's colleague's kids coming to her house to get advice from me, developed into random people I didn't know calling me for help.

I eventually began writing a book to help struggling students. I continued writing and the more I wrote, the more I enjoyed it and felt I was on to something. I would deliberately take longer train routes into work to avoid having to change onto other trains just so I could maximise my writing time. When friends were going out drinking on Friday nights, I went to the library and didn't stop writing until my eyes hurt.

I'd usually talk myself out of my own ideas and, if I didn't, my family and friends would. Many said that I should focus on trading and stop wasting time on writing. They said that it wouldn't be helpful for teenagers because 'they care about music and pop culture and not school'. There were several heated arguments with my girlfriend because she didn't believe in it either. Their words would temporarily knock my confidence, but my belief would come roaring back the next day.

Several months later, the book was published on Amazon and generated a small but steady stream of income. Then something amazing happened. I received a review from a student who used my study strategy with great success. She left a very emotional and moving review:

"I got 2 Cs a D and a B during my AS Levels. I was broken. I lost all self-confidence and had no idea how to pull my grades up. This book saved me. The revision techniques I learnt through this booked immensely helped. I was able to pull my grades up to 2 As and 1 B! I'd definitely recommend it. These techniques will stay with me for life. A bonus point was it was quite short and just really easy to read."

Reading that made me feel all warm and fuzzy inside; it still does. I couldn't stop smiling the whole day! Feedback from students produced a euphoric feeling that I'd never really experienced before. It gave me a dopamine hit that rivalled some of my most profitable trades. I didn't realise it at the time, but this was my first real dose of altruism and a key lesson that I learnt about myself.

Despite the book not making much money, I continued to work on it during evenings and weekends. Helping people provided a different type of satisfaction, and the more I helped, the more time I spent on improving book sales.

Ever since that day, the more time and money I put into the venture the more it gave back to me in both tangible and intangible returns. Tangible returns were obviously the money, while intangible returns included fulfilment from helping struggling students improve, as well as new skills like digital marketing, accounting and publishing. I learnt more about myself from this 'side project' than I did from 4 years of trading.

My love for this 'side-project' grew to the point I was neglecting my day job. Working on the book became a distraction, a procrastination. Managing partners at the firm noticed that my attention was elsewhere and voiced their concerns, but it didn't stop me.

For weeks, I lied to myself and felt guilty for working on this side project. It felt like I was cheating on my 'actual passion' which was trading. When people asked me what I did for a living I explained, 'I'm a trader and an author on the side' but really, I was an author and a trader on the side.

One day I was out with some friends and my girlfriend, when someone asked me what I did for work. I said *"I'm a derivatives trader and also write a bit on the side"*.

We spoke for about ten minutes before he left. Then my girlfriend turned to me and said, *"Why do you belittle it by calling it your side project? You spent barely half a second talking about trading, and 10 minutes talking about your mentorship programme and the book. What does that tell you?"*

A day later, I quit trading and incorporated Academic Underdogs Ltd.

Manoeuvre Yourself into a Fulfilling Career

Six months into being a business owner, the honeymoon period was over and my job consisted of an array of different tasks.

All of these were meaningful because they directly and indirectly helped students. Choosing this career path permanently ticked that box, but not all of these tasks were engaging and I was quite frankly rubbish at some.

Due to my affinity towards numbers, I was good at accounting and bookkeeping, but didn't find it engaging. It was very repetitive and offered no *variety*. Writing content was engaging, particularly when I was writing about interesting topics, but I wasn't that great at writing. As you might have noticed, I'm no J. K. Rowling.

Marketing and content creation ticked every single box. I was good at explaining processes and procedures through story telling. The whole process from start to finish was highly engaging. After creating and publishing a marketing video, an array of metrics like conversion, number of views, bounce rate etc., provided immediate *feedback*. As a business owner, I had full *autonomy* over the content I'd produce. I loved working on this part of the business.

To optimise my career further, I outsourced parts or all of the unengaging tasks that I wasn't good at. I used development editors and proofreaders to help me create written content, and hired an accountant to handle all of my bookkeeping.
I spent 20% of my time managing my contractors and the rest creating photo and video content, and digital marketing. Taking this step improved the operation of the business and, ultimately,

sales. Alas, I finally had a job that was satisfying from all angles.

What Should I Aim for in a Career?

It took me 7 years to figure out what I should prioritise in a career and to manoeuvre myself onto a path that ticked all the right boxes. Yes, starting a business gave me more control and helped me achieve this, but it can also be done when working for someone else.

One of my mentees works at an asset management firm, where she assumes a role in the financial department. She manoeuvred herself into a 'sustainable investing' job, which involved building and selling funds that only invested in ethical companies. As someone who had participated in climate change protests in the past, this was a *meaningful* place to be.

By simultaneously progressing through the management chain and building strong relationship with her superiors, she eventually secured a strategy role. This enabled her to delegate non-*engaging* grunt work to other divisions and focus on projects that she could execute well. Her life satisfaction increased, her workplace performance improved and her salary almost doubled in 3 years.

Whether you're just starting university, are an undergrad or graduate, my story should give you an idea of how this career game works. As I will emphasise many times throughout this book, optimising your life satisfaction and finding a fulfilling career is an iterative process. As someone who has found this book, you are in a great position to learn from my mistakes and secure a fulfilling career earlier than your peers.

Chapter 8
First Thing's First

Living a satisfying life with sustained fulfilment should be your ultimate aim. Given that you're probably reading this from a wealthy western country with all its support systems, your odds of achieving a high life satisfaction are good. However, it's not guaranteed and you must avoid catastrophe at all cost.

1 in 10 people in the UK have been diagnosed with severe mental disorders and this issue seems to be on the rise. Be on the right side of that statistic by simultaneously building productive habits and dampening your needs, using techniques like meditation.

As psychologists Tait, Padgett and Bladwin said; evidence indicates that job satisfaction is also moderately to strongly related to life satisfaction. Since work is a significant part of life, the correlation between work and life satisfaction makes sense—if you're happy at work you're happy at home, and vice versa. Thus, people who have jobs that they like are more likely to lead happy lives.

Making good career decisions, not only now, but for the next few decades, will deliver sustained fulfilment. Don't let your own biases distract you from the facts and if you're one of the lucky few to have found a passion for a particular career path, don't follow it blindly. Cross check your assumptions with the evidence outlined in this book.

When finding a well-suited career, the intangibles—such as meaning, engagement and ability—are more important than anything else. These should be at the forefront of your mind when seeking your optimum career path. No matter how many times I emphasise this, people continue to focus on the tangibles like money.

As you'll learn in the next chapter, income does effect happiness, but only slightly. Money is merely a tool to buy your time back and to give you control. Finding a career that ticks all the boxes can be tricky and take time because you have limited control over the tasks that you do on a day-to-day basis. Building experience and wealth enables you to customise your life and *find a meaningful and engaging career that you are good at.*

Tangibles (Money)…

Chapter 9
Does Money Buy you Happiness?

 Sterryo Official 2 weeks ago
You will be rich one day hit the like button if you agree

👍 33K 👎 REPLY

View 272 replies ⌄

Since a very young age, I assumed that I'd have a lot of money when I grew up. My friends and I would often say, *'When we are millionaires, we should...*

...rent 5 baby blue mustangs and ride up the pacific coast in America

...buy several big houses in the same neighbourhood and equip them with cinema rooms

...buy one private jet that we can all use

These were clearly just innocent dreams that every kid has, but behind them was an assumption that money could fix all problems and provide complete freedom and control. This assumption grew stronger over time. I still remember the first time I saved up my paper round money and bought expensive trainers. That dopamine rush lasted about 20 minutes.

Hundreds of experiences like these, combined with all the marketing fired at us on a daily basis, strengthens this association between money and happiness. Don't even get me started on social media, Instagram and the 'flex culture'.

There are 3 facets of money: Income, spending and wealth.

Income, Spending and Wealth

Income and spending are fairly self-explanatory, they represent the total amount of money you have coming in and going out. Wealth or 'net worth' is defined as the total you own minus the total you owe.

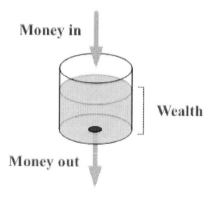

If your one and only bank balance shows £10k and you have £5k of student loan debt (you wish), your total wealth, also known as your "net worth", is £5k. That is, of course, assuming you don't own your own home or have thousands tied-up in credit card debt.

What is the Relationship Between Income and Happiness?

I have read over 20 research papers on this topic and most of them have tried to discover how income impacts life satisfaction. Researchers differ in their views, but one fact sticks out like a sore thumb: Money only buys you a significant amount of happiness when moving from poverty to stability.

In the below study, candidates with varying household incomes were assessed on their happiness and life satisfaction. They were asked various questions and scored out of 10.

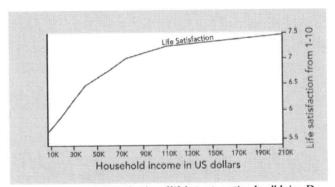

High income improves evaluation of life but not emotional well-being, D. Kahneman and A. Deaton, 2010.

Does Money Buy you Happiness?

As Kahneman and Deaton's study showed, an increase in income from $25k to $75k (£19k to £59k) resulted in approximately a 10% increase in life satisfaction; while an increase from $75k to $210k (£19k to £165k) only produced a 5% increase. Other studies have shown that beyond a £160k annual income, life satisfaction tails off; implying that, all else being equal, a person earning £500k a year has roughly the same life satisfaction as one on a £200k annual salary.

If you are earning equal to or above the average salary in your region, you would need to double your salary in order to be 5% happier. According to a study done in 2018 by the Office for National Statistics, the average salary in the UK is £27,271, which increases to £39,476 in London.

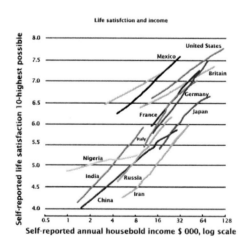

Life satisfction and income

Similar findings have been produced in other countries too. Notice how overall life satisfaction is better in wealthier countries like the UK, USA and Germany.

Annual household income on the bottom axis of the chart above is on a log scale, so the marginal increase in life satisfaction decreases the more you earn.

Diminishing returns

The richer a familt gets, the smaller the reduction in negtive emotions gained by the marginal dollar increase in household income. Gains disappear around $200,000.

Note: X axis scale is not linear.
Source: Clingigsmith (2015): Negative Emotions, Income and Welfare

In the study above, the 'reduction in negative emotions' as income increased, was analysed. Both studies highlight that money does not necessarily buy more happiness, but less money is associated with emotional pain. Low income exacerbates the emotional pain associated with such misfortunes as divorce, ill health, and loneliness.

81

Having enough money to cover all of one's physical and survival needs is a very important component of happiness. If you don't have enough wealth to feed, house, clothe, secure and educate your family, you will almost certainly be less happy than if you did.

Intimate relationships, feeling like you belong, love, friendship, and as feelings of accomplishment and self-esteem, are much *less* dependent upon (or solvable by) money. There are plenty of moderate income individuals who have warm and loving families and friends, as well as occupations or activities that provide them with strong feelings of accomplishment, even if they are not that highly compensated on an economic basis.

Ultimately, once you get enough income to be 'comfortable', having more of it really doesn't make you that much happier. It all depends on how happy you are within yourself. Beyond that, happiness is usually derived from reasons which have nothing whatsoever to do with income.

What's the Relationship Between Wealth and Happiness?

One problem with research exploring the relationship between earnings and happiness, is that most of it only looks at the money coming into each household and not the spending or total wealth of individuals. People have a tendency to spend everything they earn. Of those who earned $75k+ a year, researchers couldn't tell the difference between those who built a substantial sum of wealth and those who spent every penny.

Grant Donnelly and his team took Kahneman and Deaton's research one step further, by looking into the relationship between wealth and happiness. They found that very high levels of wealth (£6m to £12m) were associated with significantly greater happiness, and that earned wealth is associated with greater happiness than inherited wealth.

This shows that the curve does not fully flatten out at the £160k mark, as other scientists suspected, and great wealth *does* predict greater happiness.

Based on these findings, wealth does need to be considered in addition to income when considering life satisfaction, and the way in which you build that wealth matters too. Those who make it on their own are happier than those who receive it by fortune, such as winning the lottery, marrying someone wealthy or claiming an inheritance.

Additionally, researcher Richard Netemeyer found that perceived financial well-being is a key predictor of overall well-being and is comparable in magnitude to the combined effect of other life domains (job satisfaction, physical health assessment, and relationship support satisfaction).

Does Money Buy you Happiness?

Income on its own can buy you happiness, but the rate at which it continues to enhance your life slows after your salary reaches regional average levels, which is about £27k in the UK and £39k in London. After this point, wealth becomes a more prominent predictor of both happiness and life satisfaction.

Much of the research on the way that income, wealth and financial well-being relates to happiness ties into the findings mentioned in chapter 4. Wealthy people are more likely to engage in *meaningful* behaviours like volunteering and donating to charity. Many of the world's billionaires, including Warren Buffet and Bill Gates, donate most of their wealth to charity instead of passing it down to their children. They are aware that inherited wealth burdens their kids and, as Donnelly's study suggested, will most likely reduce their life satisfaction.

Wealth enables people to take greater control of their lives by giving them greater *autonomy* over how they choose to spend their time (Gallo & Mathews, 2003; Kraus, Piff, Mendoza-Denton, Rheinshmidt, & Keltner, 2012), and such feelings have been associated with higher life satisfaction.

By accumulating wealth, you can earn money passively using income producing investments (such as buying a property and renting it out). Your reliance on earning money in exchange for your time will decrease and you'll have more time to spend on activities that have a greater impact on life satisfaction. This is called *financial freedom.*

Chapter 10
Financial Freedom and why it Matters

Financial freedom is when you generate enough passive income to pay for your living expenses. *Passive income* is money you generate without investing your time.

For example, let's say that you stick £1000 in a savings account that pays you interest of 1% a month. The following month, the bank pays you £10 in interest.

That £10 is *passive income*.

On the other hand, if you work as a lawyer at an hourly rate of £300 an hour, and make £30,000 on a 100-hour contract, that £30k is *active income* because it came at the expense of your time.

Let's assume you live in central London with 3 housemates. Your monthly outgoings are as follows:

1. £1,750 on tax (this value depends on your income)
2. £700 on rent and utilities
3. £250 on transport
4. £150 on food

5. £400 for activities (including holidays)

Your total monthly expenses come to £3,250.

A distant uncle dies and leaves you an inheritance of £650,000. You stick that into another savings account, which pays you an interest of 0.5% per month. Your income is now £3,250 a month. You are technically financially free. If your expenses rise above this value and/or interest payments fall below your expenses, you're no longer financially free and will eventually need to return to work or adjust your finances accordingly.

How Much do I Need to be Financially free Forever?

Your expenses will rise as you age, especially if you live in or near a major city and want to have a family. In major cities in the UK £650,000 won't make you financially free forever. If you move to Thailand, where living costs are significantly lower, £650k will ensure you never have to work again as long as you don't invest it in something stupid.

How much do you need to be financially free forever?

I hate answering questions with 'it depends' so I'm going to give you a value you can work with. As a rule of thumb, for the average person living in the UK £1.2m will ensure financial freedom for life. At your age, this might sound like a lot but I'll show you how I came to this figure in chapter 11 and how you can save this amount well before you retire.

Assuming you live to a ripe-old age, which is quite likely as you have around an 80% chance of living to 65 years of age in the UK, financial freedom is crucial. There will be a point where your physical and mental health will prevent you from working. Even if you have kids, there is no guarantee they will be able to help you financially. The government will pay you a state pension every month, but this will only be a few hundred quid and will just about cover your basic needs.

What are the Benefits of Achieving Financial Freedom Early?

You don't need to wait until the age of 65 before achieving financial freedom. People can, and do, get there early. This can have many positive benefits.

Here's a conversation I had with Rajiv, an acquaintance from university who became financially free aged just 36:

Me: *"How did you become financially free at such a young age?"*

Rajiv: *"I saved a big chunk of my salary for several years, then I used my savings to invest in property. I also got a little lucky by betting on some cryptocurrencies. Living a fairly frugal life helps as well."*
Me: *"What portion of your net worth would you say came from your crypto-bets?"*

Rajiv: *"Around 15%. I didn't invest much but it gave me confidence to start investing."*

Me: *"Are you happier now that you are financially free?"*

Rajiv: *"I would say so, yes."*

Me: *"Why?"*

Rajiv: *"A number of reasons, but mostly because I have less anxiety concerning work and money."*

Me: *"Go on..."*

Rajiv: *"While working, I always had this underlying fear that I'd be laid off and wouldn't have a way to pay my rent. Also, I'd often worry about the embarrassment of being called into my manager's office and being told to leave. I'd think about stuff like this quite often and still do worry about money, but nowhere near as much as I did before."*

Me: *"Did it affect your relationships?"*

Rajiv: *"I spend time with whoever I want to now. In the corporate world, sometimes you feel the need to be fake or hold back the truth just to avoid ruining your reputation. I don't need to do that anymore and it's a massive weight off my shoulders."*

Me: *"That would definitely be something I'd love!"*

Rajiv: *"It also makes you stop hating on the government so much. When you're working hard or running a business, you gradually start resenting the government for taking more and more money away from you. I still pay relatively high taxes but don't mind so much now because I haven't had to put myself through so much stress to earn it."*

Me: *"Is there anything else?*

Rajiv: *"Time, I'd say. A few of my friends are in the same boat as me and we live with much more freedom than most people we know. For example, I've spent about 7 weeks travelling with them over the past year. We don't spend big—we mostly stay in hostels and Airbnbs—but we would never have 7 weeks free if we were employed."*

Me: *"Is there a downside to achieving financial freedom?*

Rajiv: *"When I left my job, there was a period of a few months where I became bored and miserable. Having choice and free time can be overwhelming when you've been on the go for several years. After I got a routine and some structure back into my life, it all improved! Everything has been great ever since."*

Me: *"How do you spend your time now?"*

Rajiv: *"I invest in and work with a lot of social enterprises and companies that deliver social impact. I often mentor founders* *and step in to do work I enjoy like raising capital and structuring deals. "*

Whether you achieve financial freedom on or before your retirement age, there is no guarantee you'll be happy. You will still need to invest your time into worthwhile activities and spend time with people who make you feel good. Financial freedom offers you more choice and freedom, what you do with that choice is up to you.

Some of the happiest people I know are financially free and use their spare time productively. They take care of their physical health by eating correctly and exercising. Most of them take care of their mental health by meeting friends and family regularly; a few meditate every day. They self-actualise in their free time using hobbies or projects of varying size and nature.

When and How Should you Achieve Financial Freedom?

If you get a job and don't save or receive a lump sum of money, the government will define when you achieve financial freedom. This will most likely be at the age of 65, although it's steadily increasing. Our social and welfare system is designed to encourage us to become financially free after that age because if we're not, the government has to cover the costs.
If you want to achieve financial freedom before 65, you will need to build up a lump sum of money. There are several ways you can do this and we'll discuss those ways in the next few chapters.

Financial Freedom and why it Matters

Chapter 11
How to be Financially Free in 6 Months

Financial freedom should be the ultimate goal for every single one of us. It can have a directly positive impact on our happiness and it can indirectly improve our health, longevity, and satisfaction. If you earn money while you sleep, play and exercise, then you can spend more time focusing on the things that matter and less time worrying about your role in the rat race.

It only makes sense, but achieving financial freedom is neither simple nor easy and the very thing that it helps us to escape is the thing we need to achieve it.

As you can imagine, going from £0 to £1m+ quickly is an unbelievably difficult and risky task. Making this amount of money in one fell swoop often requires a massive stroke of luck, like winning the lottery or marrying a millionaire.

So how can you do it? Well, unfortunately, there is no teachable way to make that kind of money in such a short period of time. You can rob a bank, wait for a rich relative to die or win the lottery, but I wouldn't recommend any of those things.

You may have come across some social media gurus who have claimed to make huge sums of money in a short period of time and promise to help you do the same. I've worked with some of these gurus myself and can tell you with absolute confidence that 99.9% of them are talking out of their backsides.

The problem is, preaching about making millions is not more profitable than actually making millions. Anyone who claims to be making $200k+ a day using a certain set of techniques and then spends all their time trying to sell you these techniques for a few bucks, is either a liar or an idiot.

The world doesn't work that way. Sure, some people got very lucky after taking massive risks and being funded by the Bank of Mum and Dad, but it's not something you can easily emulate, nor is it something you should even try to emulate.

If becoming financially free is something which looks good to you, then you need to understand that it won't come easy, it won't come quickly, and anyone promising either of those things is a charlatan who will only make you poorer.

Chapter 12
How to be Financially Free in 10 Years

You can't achieve financial freedom in 6 months or a year. We've established that. However, if you want to achieve this in years to come then you will need to start now. It is possible to become financially free by the time you reach 30 years of age. It's not easy, and it's not common either, but it is possible.

Of all the people I know who have achieved this, most of them made their first £1m using an early inheritance or loan from their parents to start a business. The rest came via high paying jobs and disciplined spending.

There are four realistic ways that you can make your first six-figure sum by the time you hit 30:

1. High Salary Jobs

A high salary job is one that offers a starting salary equal to or above the average, while also providing exponential career growth. For example:

1. Investment banking, particularly the 'front-office' functions like sales and trading.

2. Law, especially at firms in major cities.

3. Engineering, mainly offshore oil and gas process engineers.

4. Management consulting at top 3 or 4 global companies.

Secure a job in one of these industries and your earnings will be in the top 10% of your cohort right out of university. Your income may be above that 'life satisfaction threshold' straight away, but you may need a few years to reach that level.

So, what's the catch?

Firstly, these jobs are very competitive. Graduates can't resist the allure of these high salaries and impressive brand names, and understandably so—having these company names on your CV adds more value than your university degree. Even if you work at one these firms for just a few months, you will gain a significant edge over someone who doesn't. When I told people that I worked at an investment bank, their eyes widened and their interest in me suddenly shot up. This felt good for a short period of time but it was superficial. Social status should not enter your decision-making process when choosing a career.

Secondly, if you do get through the door, stereotypes suggest you will be 'selling your soul' in some way shape or form. It will cost you time, stress and health (both physical and mental). You'll feel like a small cog in a massive wheel. These career paths could lack the altruistic feel good elements of other career paths like medicine or teaching. This is the intangible price you pay for the tangible boost in income.

Thirdly, you can become trapped very easily with 'golden handcuffs'. Very often, people join these companies on graduate training programmes and never leave their industries for decades. This never made sense to me—surely, if you make £1,600,000 after tax over 20 years, £600,000 goes into your living expenses and £1,000,000 in savings and investments. Through compounding returns, this £1,000,000 would be £1,300,000 by the time you hit 40. At this stage, you would no longer need to sell your soul every day and can find a more meaningful career path. Parking that £1,300,000 into a diversified portfolio could return around 5% or £65,000 per year.

With this amount of *passive income* someone could quit their job, stick the kids in a grammar school, live frugally and self-actualise. If their kids need to be in private schools or they want to travel, they just need to work a few days a week.

In reality, people become trapped by their spending habits and they don't save or invest. They do things like invest in Bitcoin or in a friend's business that has little to no chance of working; they stick to brands and play fast and loose with their direct debits; they don't compare car insurance or utility service quotes each year. Small losses like this add up to large ones over the course of several years.

This was the path I was heading down during university until I realised that something didn't smell right and I pivoted away. I found that other, less competitive career paths exist which offer similar income and career growth without all the impressive status stuff, but with an added risk.

I call these commission paying jobs.

2. Commission Paying Jobs

Recruiters, estate agents, medical sales representatives, proprietary traders—these are jobs which have lower than average base salaries, but offer performance based commissions. Many of these jobs require an undergraduate degree.

Recruiters are middle men between companies and candidates. When a company wants to hire a new sales manager, for example, they will call a recruitment agency and ask them to find someone who can do the job. You, as the recruiter, have to scour LinkedIn and the company database to find the right fit. After finding a few suitable candidates, you need to convince them to go for that job and facilitate the hiring process. If one of your candidates is hired, your company receives a nice big fee, sometimes equivalent to 100% of the candidate's annual salary of which you get a commission.

One particular recruitment agent in the city of London offers a starting salary of around £20k with very little scope to earn more during the first year. As you learn more about the business and become more experienced, you earn commissions based on the number of candidates you place at new companies. These commissions can double your base salary depending on the clients you have, the industry you are hiring in and, most importantly, your ability to sell.

If you are in the top 10% of performers, your compensation can be between £75-100k (£25-30k base salary & £50-70k commission). This can be double the amount of someone working in some high-paying low-risk jobs. From year 4 onwards, a top 10% performer can earn £100k+ a year, which is better than some highly competitive jobs. And they don't need to sell their soul to get there!

So, what's the catch?

If you aren't in the top 30% of performers, your compensation will be below the 'life-satisfaction threshold' and you will feel the pinch. Companies that offer this commission structure deliberately keep their base salaries low to incentivise employees to focus on commissions. They make more money doing it this way.

This is why some of these commission based jobs are risky. If Peter is capable of earning £120k over 3 years in a low-risk job, by going for a high-risk job with a base of £90k over 3 years, he is risking £30k of potential earnings for higher rewards. In my opinion, when working one of these jobs, you should aim to make at least 3 times your 'at risk' earnings. Peter should be aiming to make £180k over 3 years to justify his risk. If he doesn't achieve that, retraining or creating additional income would be the best move.

From a purely financial perspective, if you have the gift of the gab then risking 2 or 3 years in a commission role is a sound decision.

Most commission jobs are sales orientated. However, some unconventional career paths like proprietary trading don't require sales skills at all and are incredibly high risk. The firm I joined offered no salary and my compensation was entirely dependent on my performance. My job involved a lot of analytics and pattern recognition. As I mentioned earlier, it was almost like a computer game. In other industries, the top 20% can stay above the 'life satisfaction threshold' but in my job only the top 5% could hope to achieve this.

Given that I was securing final round interviews for roles offering £42k base salary right out of university rising to £58k by year 3, my total 'at risk salary' was £159,000. I was risking this amount of money with the intention to make £639,000 by year 4. Unfortunately, my risk didn't pay off, I became miserable, and I had to pivot into my education and book business.

3. Early Inheritance

Asking your family members for an early inheritance, loan or financial gifts to supplement your income is an easy way to reach the 'life satisfaction threshold' quickly. This option is obviously only reserved for those who have parents that have enough wealth to give.

In my opinion, you should avoid relying on gifts from parents. It's their money—they've worked hard to make it and have probably sacrificed a lot to get there.

From a practical standpoint, accepting cash gifts will also impact your spending habits. There is something inherently satisfying about using your time and creativity to make your own money. As discussed in chapter 9, empirical evidence shows that earned income is a better predictor of happiness than unearned income.

It's a different story if you ask for an investment or loan and you use that money to start a business. In this case you're not asking for handouts, you're not begging them to make your life easier by buying you out of debt or into a new car/house. You're simply asking them to fund a venture that can give you a head-start and allow you to make your own fortune

Someone I know asked his parents for a £300,000 loan to start his own real estate business, renovating and then selling dilapidated properties. He made £180k over 3 years, well above the 'life satisfaction threshold', and paid back his parents with interest a few years later. He now makes £100k a year from working 20 hours a week at the age of 28. The rest of the time he plays cricket, exercises, and socialises with friends and family.

If all parties understand the risks involved and you put the effort in to learn the business, it can be a great approach. Of course, £300,000 is a lot of money and not everyone has access to family funding like this, but there are other options.

4. Start a Business

Fuelled by the media's coverage of celebrity entrepreneurs like Mark Zuckerberg and Elon Musk, interest in technology and entrepreneurship has risen exponentially over the last 10 years. Businesses run by students in the UK generate £1bn a year in revenue and one in ten graduates start a business straight after university. One in every four graduates plan to start their own company at some point in the future.

Unfortunately, graduates make a lot of false assumptions about entrepreneurship and don't go into it with their eyes open. When people think about entrepreneurs, they think about two guys building a product in their garage and growing the value of their company into ridiculous sums of money. This is partially true. Entrepreneurship is about ownership of a company and a company is a group of people who have aligned goals. However, to be an owner, you don't need to start from 0 in your garage.

You could join an existing start-up and be compensated with shares or a combination of shares and salary. For example, Emma Apple Crisps, a vegetable and fruit crisp company, has 10 employees and has raised £1,000,000 in funding. If they like the look of you, they offer you £20,000 salary with £20,000 worth of stock options per year as a compensation package.

After your first year, you will own 0.5% of Emma Fruit Crisps and will have earned £20,000. If the company does well, the value of the company and your shares will increase. Let's say after 5 years, Emma Fruit Crisps are stocked in Tesco's nation-wide and have expanded internationally. Your ownership of the company has gone up to 2% and is worth £200,000. This means you have made around £300,000 in 5 years with the potential to earn more in the future as the value of Emma goes up. Not bad!

Of course, if the company doesn't win the Tesco contract, or fails to expand internationally and then fails, your shares will be worthless and you'll only have made £100,000. Not great! This is the bet that you take by joining someone else's start-up. Launching your own business is even riskier.

There are a bunch of low-barrier-to-entry businesses you can start right after university. These are usually 'proven business models' that many other people are already doing and typically don't require large capital investments. They include online E-commerce businesses like selling physical products on Amazon or eBay, as well as offline businesses like property development or opening an Italian restaurant on a high street.

High-barrier-to-entry businesses usually don't have proven business models and have very few people trying—such as a company that sells lab-grown diamonds online or a business that manufactures robotic bartenders. With these ventures, you need to find both the team members and the money to launch. As a fresh graduate, this is possible but very difficult.

Even though the media talk about how 19 year olds make billions of pounds starting high-barrier-to-entry ventures from their parents' garage, being an entrepreneur isn't for everyone. Only a tiny fraction of those who start businesses actually go on to build these unicorn companies worth more than a billion pounds. About 5% become wealthy, 10% do OK, 20% do no better than if they were employed. As for the rest, they fail miserably.

Also, most founders of these high growth companies are around 40 years old, as shown by the graph below. For the 1 out of 4 graduates who don't start businesses after university but intend to do so later, getting a job for 5-7 years first is sound judgement, even though it goes against the media narrative.

The vast majority of founders have experience in their domain. With that in mind, consider staying in university and getting a job for 5–7 years—become amazing in your field and *then* start your own business.

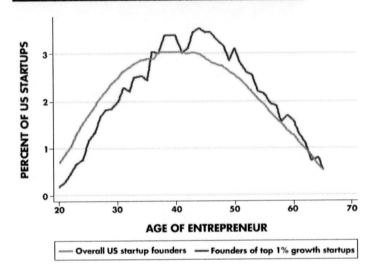

FOUNDER AGE DISTRIBUTION:
ALL STARTUPS AND HIGH-PERFORMANCE STARTUPS

Overall US startup founders ——— Founders of top 1% growth startups

If you start a high-barrier-to-entry venture after university, the odds of success will be stacked against you. It will take you time to raise investment and if you do, it's unlikely that you'll draw much salary for yourself over the first few years. Even if you satisfy the first two levels of Maslow's hierarchy, you'll have very little time to spend with friends and family.

You'll be miserable and will need to take extra care of your mental health.

As discussed already, some people are made to be entrepreneurs and others just don't have what it takes. You need a certain drive and ambition—you need to be creative, to take risk. If you are this type of person then you will have understood everything I've said above.

An entrepreneur won't care about the odds. They back their ability and would rather try and fail than not try at all. Is that you? If so, then by all means, take a crack at it but do it with your eyes open, understand what your bet is and work like you've never worked before.

If you have a strong affinity or desire to be an entrepreneur, working first, acquiring experience and then starting a business is a safer bet than going knee-deep into a new industry. Starting a side hustle would be the next best thing, then after gaining some understanding and testing your main assumptions, you can take the leap.

Starting a business right out of university with limited mentorship and experience, is a higher risk option.

How to be Financially Free in 10 Years

If you have the minimum grade requirements and the gift of the gab, going for a high-risk high-reward industry with big bonuses would be a great option. You'll probably be good at it so you will enjoy parts of the job and will achieve financial freedom early.

If you're not that good with numbers but can sell, try a commission based job like recruitment consulting. You will know where you stand by year 3.

Whatever decision you choose, proceed with your eyes open, and try to understand what you are losing and what you are gaining.

Chapter 13
How to be Financially Free in 20+ Years

If you don't have a burning desire to start your own business or to join a start-up, getting a 'normal' salaried job with 'normal' working hours is a sustainable way of living. This is what the majority of the population do and traditionally it's the role that many of us are primed for throughout our lives. However, whenever I speak to those in this group, they are not happy and they feel unaccomplished. They feel like this is them for the rest of their lives and that no matter what they do, they are always destined to be stuck in a dead-end job until they retire aged 65 or 70.

But it's not all doom and gloom. Anybody with a £30,000-£40,000 job can become financially free by 40 or 50 by maximising their earnings, having good spending habits, investing, and not taking any big risks. The academic evidence is quite clear on that.

Not breaking your back for 60+ hours a week will ensure you have some evenings and weekends free to decompress. If you enjoy your job, or part of it; you do your best to secure promotions where possible and to make sound investments when you have the chance, you can retire before you hit 50.

That "normal" job doesn't sound so bad now, does it? Here's how you can retire early with salaried work like this.

How to Become a Millionaire on an Average Salary

Salah is a 40-year-old millionaire who began his career selling double-glazing. It began as a part-time job to help him through university, but he accepted a full-time position after graduating because he couldn't be bothered to find anything else. He was earning £26,000 to begin with and this was subsidised by regular sales commissions and a frugal lifestyle.

Me: *"Sorry if I'm coming across blunt, how did you become a millionaire starting on that salary?"*

Salah: *"I appreciate your frankness and feel free to be as blunt as you want. Ultimately, it came down to being disciplined with my finances and investing regularly."*

Me: *"Go on..."*

Salah: *"I started by asking friends and family and then read a few books about how to build wealth. There are so many people out there who claim to have the best way to become wealthy and they're all convincing. Many claim to have a track record or proof, but when you ask them details about it, they become flaky and unresponsive."*

Me: *"How did you know who to trust?"*

Salah: *"There were some advisors I came across who stood out for the right reasons. A handful of them weren't flaky when I asked them for details. They presented both sides of the argument clearly and justified their conclusions using peer reviewed studies. They never sold me anything. I never heard phrases like 'there is zero risk here' or 'this is a guaranteed way of earning £x in y years'. Whenever I asked to see proof of their claims, they sent back several bullet points and accompanying academic research. I developed my strategy and 3 rules based on these sources."*

Salah's core rules were:

1. Save as much as possible.
2. Invest your savings in stock and bond index funds.
3. Don't invest in opportunities that lack evidence.

FTSE 100, S&P 500, DAX—these are all names of *stock* indexes. The FTSE 100 contains the largest 100 companies traded on the London Stock Exchange, while the S&P 500 is a list of the top 500 companies in the USA.

By investing in a stock index fund, you are essentially buying a small piece of every company in that index. If the collective value of those companies goes up, you make money. If they go down, you lose money.

Bonds are loan agreements. When you buy a bond, you are loaning a company or government a certain amount of money. In exchange, they pay you a fixed interest payment just like a bank. By investing money into a *Government Bond Index Fund*, you are essentially lending money to every government listed in that index and they are paying you interest.

Salah calculated that if he invested 30-40% of his salary every year for 15 years, he would have a net worth of around £800,000 by age 40. All he needed to do was follow his 3 rules and his finances would be taken care of, leaving him with more time to focus on more important areas like relationships and health.

Me: *"Seems pretty simple. Why doesn't everyone do it?"*

Salah: *"There are millions of people who use some variation of this strategy right now."*

Me: *"Who?"*

Salah: *"Anyone who has a pension. Do you have a pension?"*

Me: *"Yes."*

Salah: *"Where is your pension money invested at this moment in time?"*
Me: *"Half of it is in a FTSE 100 index tracker fund and the rest in government bonds."*

Salah: *"I think you should change that ratio but we can talk about that later. But you just proved my point, even you are* *using this strategy. The only difference is that, in addition to investing 1-2% of my salary into my pension pot, I invested an additional 40+% of my income into my personal investment pot. I did this for 20 years."*

Me: *"It still sounds really simple—almost too simple."*

Salah: *"I felt the same way in the beginning. It feels as though becoming financially free should be complex or require rigorous intelligence. When you think of wealthy people like Bill Gates or Mark Zuckerberg, they all seem to have super intelligence and amazing ideas. It's easy to assume that only people in that league can become wealthy but it's not true. Plenty of people build wealth by developing good habits and sticking to them for many years. Saving is the most important habit of them all."*

Me: *"Were you a good saver?"*

Salah: *"Initially, no. Six months after showing my financial plan to my very sceptical uncle—a successful investor—he asked me how much I had saved so far. My answer was '-£800'. My account was in overdraft and he rolled his eyes."*

Me: *"What happened?"*

Salah: *"Saving is a habit and it's easier to form this habit from a young age. Whoever invented the piggy bank for kids is a ge-*

nius—I would shake his hand if he was still alive! After under-standing the psychology behind saving and developing the cor-rect saving habits, my path to financial freedom became much clearer."

Saving More

Income – Expenses = Savings

To save you need to earn more than you spend. Simple and ob-vious. However, most people struggle to save regularly because it's much easier to spend than it is to earn. Buying a £100 jacket that you don't need takes a couple minutes but the average UK worker needs to work 5 to 10 hours to earn that amount. Unfor-tunately, our brains crave the quick dopamine hit that spending provides and prefer this over a sustained release provided by earning. This affects everyone regardless of how much you earn.

Salah: *"One of my friends was a high-flying investment banker who earned £50,000 straight out of university and was on six figures by the time he reached 26. He worked 80 hours a week. My net worth is five times his now."*

Me: *"How?! Surely he must have been making hundreds of thousands of pounds by the time he reached 30?"*

Salah: *"He had an unbelievably good salary but his spending habits were terrible. For example, he once bought a car brand* *new while I bought a similar model for £15,000 less in an auction. His home insurance was auto renewed every year for the past 20 years. This cost him an additional £12,000!"*

Me: *"Surely these were all small costs compared to his enormous salary?"*

Salah: *"Yes, but they all add up!"*

David James (England footballer), 50 Cent, Johnny Depp, Mike Tyson and Nicholas Cage are just a few high profile high earners who went bankrupt after earning millions of pounds. Michael Jackson made over a billion dollars over the course of his career but died practically penniless.

All these individuals were able to practice self-discipline in their particular areas of craft. David James would never have become a top footballer if he wasn't able to train consistently over many years. Unfortunately, being disciplined in one area of your life doesn't guarantee that you will do the same in another. That's why it's important to educate yourself on all the critical areas that affect your fulfilment. These include personal finance, emotional wellbeing, career, relationships and health.

Some of the world's best fitness and weight loss instructors emphasise that diet is more important than exercise. You can control 100% of what goes into your mouth but only around 10-20% of the calories you burn through exercise. It takes no time to pick up a chocolate bar over an apple, but burning the 300 calories from that bar requires an hour of running. This is deceivingly disproportionate.

In theory, if you have a semi-decent job, saving should be easy because we have 100% control over what we spend. You can choose a £10 a month phone contract or a £40 a month one; a £100 a week flat share or a £250 a week let; a £5 meal deal at Pizza Express or a £12 Chicken and Chips at Nandos.

You have much less choice when it comes to your earnings. No one will hand you a catalogue of jobs outlining the intangibles and salary and then give you the freedom to cherry-pick your favourites. You are limited by a number of factors including your time and skills, not to mention that you have much less control over your competition for any given job or the employer's opinion of you. On the job, you have no control over the performance of the company as a whole or the budgeting decisions made by your superiors.

This disproportionality and our control over our spending versus our earning is why some of the world's most successful money managers emphasise the importance of managing your expenses above all else. Start with what you *can* control and build from there.

How do I Spend Less?

"Can I achieve the same or similar result without spending money?"

Whenever I am faced with a choice to spend, this is the first question I ask myself. Over the course of the last few years, I've probably asked myself this question hundreds of thousands of times.

Yesterday, a salesperson from a newly refurbished gym called me to offer 50% off their annual membership. He was a brilliant salesperson and had me sold by the end of the conversation, but despite his pressure to close, I held back from making a decision until later (another habit) and when I hung-up the phone I thought it through.

Me 1: *"Can I achieve the same or similar result without spending money?"*

Me 2: *"I go to the gym to keep my body-fat percentage below 15% (tangible) and to feel good (intangible). Last year, I dropped my body-fat percentage from 22% to 12% doing home video workouts in my garage, for free. If I have done it for free in the past, I can do it for free again. No deal."*

Another question I tend to ask myself is:

"What am I losing and what am I gaining?"
One of my friends was offered a brand-new iPhone by her employer which combined her current personal and work phones into one device.

Me: *"What are you losing and what are you gaining?"*

116

Friend: *"I am gaining an additional £30 a month as they are paying for both my personal and business phone contracts. So, that's £360 (tangible) a year in my pocket. I am losing my relaxation time (intangible).*

At least now, I can leave my work phone at home when I want to go for dinner and don't hear that e-mail notification sound. Although, I could just turn those off after I leave work and be more self-disciplined when checking my phone. I'm taking the deal."

Laying your decisions out like this helps you think clearly and act fast. Mulling over small financial decisions, however, makes no sense, you're better off using that time to do something else. By asking yourself these questions you will naturally develop good spending habits. This is how *gradualism* works.

gradualism
noun
1. a policy of gradual reform rather than sudden
   change or revolution.

Thinking critically and nudging yourself into good habits across all areas of your life will result in significant changes over the long term.

One of the habits I've had for over 15 years is reading immediately after waking up. This has helped me accumulate more information and provided a clear understanding of some of the most complex areas in life. Friends and colleagues often ask me, "How the hell do you know all that?".

Another habit I have developed through gradualism is healthy eating. As I'm writing now in Starbucks, I see people eating pastries and paninis all over the place. I haven't ordered or even been tempted to order any coffee shop food for the past decade. I only order coffee, usually an Americano which barely has any calories.

I'm sure you also have areas of your life where you are more disciplined than others, but it's something that can apply to everything you do and something that will greatly improve your life when it does. Continuously use critical thinking to cultivate your decision making and become a little better every day. Sooner or later, people will start asking you questions like, 'How are you so disciplined with your work or health or personal finances?'. You won't know how to answer that question because years of gradualism enabled you to make the correct decisions instinctively.

Another habit that will help you save is to simply not be afraid to ask for things.

"Can you put me through to your manager?"

or

"Sorry that's above my budget, can you do anything on the price?"

or

"I've received another quote for £x, but your reviews are better. So, I'd rather go with you, if you can match their price."

That last line is very effective at getting you high-value services at a discount. Always ask, even when it feels a little uncomfortable and *especially* when dealing with large corporations.

How do I Earn More?

Not only will a little communication go a long way when asking for discounts, but it could also secure a raise. You don't get if you don't ask, as the saying goes.

Negotiating pay rises at work is the easiest way to increase your earnings without risking any additional time or money. A £5,000 increase in your salary can result in hundreds of thousands of pounds in future savings.
Unfortunately, asking for more money, especially from your employer, can be very uncomfortable, particularly if you have grown up in the UK. It feels greedy. I personally know several individuals who are excellent at their jobs but still feel uncomfortable asking for promotions and pay rises.

Remember that your contract with your employer is a two-way deal. You are giving your time and expertise in exchange for money. How much you deserve for your time is subjective and you shouldn't be afraid to have an opinion on what your time is worth. Your employer has no qualms about sharing their views on your value. Even if you are a modest person, you should *__always__* ask.

Be sure to do your research before entering a negotiation. There is a lot of information out there on negotiation tactics, so I won't go into detail, but the main points are as follows:

1. As a rule of thumb, you are far more likely to receive a pay rise by moving to another firm rather than staying with the one you're in.

2. Interview with other companies regularly, preferably once every two years. This helps you keep your CV up-to-date and give you interview experience.

3. Use personal contacts and online resources like Glassdoor to check salaries paid by your company. Recruitment agents can also be very helpful.

4. Entering a salary negotiation with other, stronger job offers puts you at a great advantage. You don't need to bluff and can walk away if you're not happy with your compensation package. It's a win-win.

5. Know what you want before going into the negotiation and define your 'walk away' price.

6. Anticipate objections and rehearse your responses.

7. Understand your own biases. We tend to negotiate less with people we like, so keep this in mind if you get along well with your manager

8. Understand the full package. It's not all about take home pay. What is the culture like, do the benefits suit you?

All of the above is applicable to negotiating severance pay too. This is when a corporation pays you several months or sometimes years of salary in one go, usually when they want you to leave the company. Check out a book called, 'Never Split the Difference' by an ex-FBI negotiator before you enter your next high-stakes negotiation.

Me: *"Let's take a graduate who is earning £30,000 a year. How can they achieve financial freedom like you?"*

Salah: *"They should first save 3 months of salary in a bank account just in case they lose their job. Then, they should invest a minimum of 20% of their monthly salary in stock and bond index funds. 18% in stocks and 2% in bonds. If they save £20 after month 1, £18 should go into a stock index fund and £2 in a bond fund."*

Put your Money in Index and Bond Funds

Salah's suggestion is in line with many successful investors, including Warren Buffet, America's most successful investor. By placing most of your money into a stock index fund, you are betting that the largest companies in the world will become more efficient and valuable over the next 20+ years. There is 200 years' worth of data justifying this bet.

£10,000 invested in the FTSE All-Share Index in 1985 would now be worth £129,128 as of May 2019. This is a 1191% return on your investment! Placing that £10,000 in the USA, Canadian or other European stock indexes would have also generated a fantastic return. Placing it in a bank account earning interest would have left you with around £30,000.

Salah started investing in 1998 at the age of 20. He saved 36% of his total annual salary in his first year; a total of £9,397. After opening an account with his financial advisor, he invested £8,457 in a FTSE All-Share Index Tracker Fund and £940 in a global government bond tracker fund. One year later, he received a statement saying that the total value of his investment went up to £10,583.

Me: *"That must have felt good!"*

Salah: *"Yes, it did. The stock markets went up that year. All the companies in the FTSE All-Share Index collectively increased in value by around 10% and they paid a dividend of around*

122

3%. Then the bonds paid out around 2%. I kicked myself for not saving more!"

Me: *"What did you do next?"*

Salah: *"Seeing that profit really inspired me so I sorted out all my finances. I cut my spending right down and negotiated a higher sales commission with my employer. I received my salary on the 20th of the month and £1,250 was sent immediately to my financial advisor by direct debit. I earned around £34k that year and saved £15k."*

Me: *"I'm surprised by how much you managed to save. Your expenses came to £19k that year which is £1.6k a month. Was it difficult to live under that budget?"*

Salah: *"Out of the £2.8k I earned each month, about £500 went to the tax man and £1,250 to my financial advisor. This left me with £1,110 per month which was enough to cover my living expenses and £500 a month for 'fun money'. I still went on holidays and ate out with my friends, but I cut my spending in other areas. For example, I didn't own a car for a while and went to a £5 barber instead of a £15 one."*

That year global stock markets went up again and the FTSE All-Share Index went up 24.2%. Salah's end of year statement showed a £32,141. By the end of year 2, Salah earned himself £7,001 in his sleep!

Me: *"What happened in year 3?"*

Salah: *"The FTSE All-Share Index went down and so did the value of my investment pot. I think it was down by about £2,000."*

Me: *"Were you nervous?"*

Salah: *"Not at first, then over the course of the year I heard a lot of negative sentiment in the news. There were headlines about the 'dot-com bubble bursting' and financial gurus were talking about it going down even further."*

Me: *"Did you get your money out?"*

Salah: *"No I stuck with it for the whole year, but then in 2002, the stock market tanked another 25% - I s*** myself! I wanted to get my cash out before it went down further then maybe buy it back a year later at a lower price. Before calling my financial advisor, I ran my plan by my uncle."*

Me: *"What did he say?"*

Salah: *"He told me to stop being an idiot and remind myself of the evidence—those were his exact words."*

Me: *"Haha!"*

Salah: *"In his lifetime, he'd seen the stock market fall 30%+ several times. On one occasion, he'd seen his investment account go from £1,400,000 to £960,000 in 6 months! Over the past 200 years, stock markets have gone up and they will most likely continue to go up but it will always be a bumpy ride."*

Me: *"So he told you to keep your cash in there and ride out the crash?"*

Salah: *"Yes. Crashes are inevitable and there can also be several years of stagnant growth. It's very important that you ignore the noise and the 'gurus' on TV. Studies have shown that 98% of these gurus and DIY investors who try to dance in and out of the markets, to buy low and sell high, actually make less money than those who hold their investments long term. That 2% who can consistently 'time the markets' are usually very sophisticated investors who spend millions of pounds on research."*

Salah listened to his uncle and kept his investments in place. As expected, the global markets, including the FTSE All-Share Index, went up for several years after the crash and his discipline paid off.

Salah continued to improve his spending habits, worked hard at his job and negotiated pay rises over the next few years. He managed to invest around 40% of his salary over this period. At the age of 30, he was earning £63k per year and his investment account had grown to £268,793.

If he hadn't invested any of his savings and kept all of it under his mattress, Salah would have had £193,791. If he had kept it in a bank account earning interest he would have had £231,743. In the end, he earned himself £75,002 (£268,793 (invested income), and £193,791 (non-invested income) from pretty much doing nothing.

Me: *"You really didn't take any cash out or tamper with the investment over those 10 years?"*

Salah: *"Once a year I'd rebalance the investments so that I had the correct ratio of 90% Stocks and 10% Bonds. That's all I did."*

In 2008, when Salah turned 31, the global stock markets crashed again and he saw his investment account go from a high of £308,802 down to £255,683. He held firm again and continued to invest for the next 10 years. At the age of 39, his investment account stood at a whopping £1,061,438.

The graph below shows how this investment strategy grew his wealth over 20 years (top line). It also shows how his wealth would have grown had he put all his savings in a bank account (middle line) and as cash under his mattress (bottom line).

INVESTING VS SAVINGS BANK ACCOUNT VS CASH UNDER THE MATTRESS

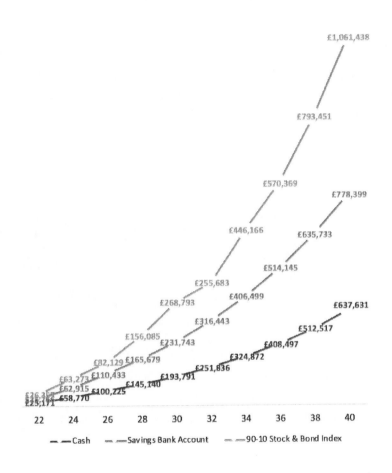

Me: *"Your wealth grew exponentially over the past few years, why is that?"*

Salah: *"This was partly because I was able to save more as my salary increased. But, most of this acceleration was created by the 'compounding affect'."*

Compounding is when you make gains from previous gains. Think of it as a snowball rolling down a snowy hill. The larger the ball gets, the more snow it takes on—that's compounding. Many successful investors, including Warren Buffet, have used compounding to create sizeable fortunes.

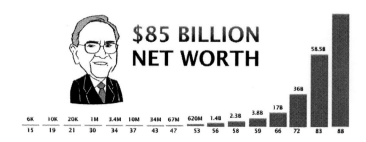

50% of Salah's wealth was generated in the last 4 years, while the other 50% took 16 years to build. This is typical when you compound and it's why it's so hard for a 19 or 20-year-old to visualise themselves becoming a millionaire on an average salary.

Me: *"During this whole time, were you not tempted to invest your money into something else?"*

Salah: *"All the time!"*

Don't Make Bad Investments

From time to time, Salah's friends encouraged him to invest in various opportunities that had earned them money. These included a football spread betting strategy, a network marketing programme selling fitness products, gold bullion trading and cryptocurrencies. Each time, his uncle reminded him of the evidence and encouraged him not to participate.

Salah: *"I was very close to buying Bitcoin when it was trading near its peak. Thankfully I didn't! This is when it helps to have a decent mentor like my uncle who kept reminding me of the evidence and to stay disciplined. After he told me off again, I re-read a lot of my investment books and completely tore up the idea of investing in cryptocurrencies"*

There are millions of ways to invest and almost just as many people advising you on *where* to invest. As you start earning a salary, investment opportunities and money-making schemes will land in your inbox and appear on your news feeds. Friends and family will start advising you, either because they want you to invest in their business, or because they want to recommend something that worked for them. Some of these might make you a lot of money in the short-term, however, they are unlikely to generate the same return that stock markets do over the long-term.

Salah: *"Will block chain technology revolutionise the way we transact with each other? Maybe. Will Bitcoin go to $50,000? Who knows? The truth is, it's all speculation. No one really knows. All I know is that the global stock markets have gone up for 200 years while Bitcoin has been around for a fraction of that time. To me, the former is a better bet until someone proves otherwise."*

Why Doesn't Everyone do this?

According to the Institute of Fiscal Studies, having a net worth of over £1m puts Salah in the top 2% of the UK population.

Percentile plot of total household wealth per adult

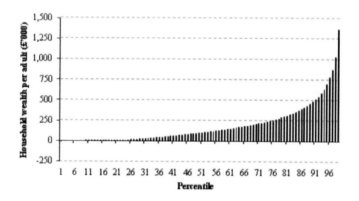

There is nothing revolutionary about Salah's investment strategy. So why haven't the other 90% of the population done it? For starters, many don't know much about personal finances or investment because money is not the most interesting topic of conversation. If you see a book about 'Value Investing' next to Harry Potter, which one would you go for?

Of those who do educate themselves, not everyone can come to terms with the processes and many don't have the discipline to save. Developing and then maintaining those saving habits can be tricky. The rest either struggle to hold their nerve during crashes, or allow themselves to be roped into various money-making opportunities.

Knowing what to do isn't enough. There are doctors out there who are overweight and smoke; lawyers who get into legal issues. I'm sure there are a fair few financial advisors who don't follow their own advice as well. Continuous and sustained execution is the key to building wealth.

Me: *"So, as of now, are you financially free?"*

Salah: *"I'm married with 2 children and for us to be completely financially free, I'd need around £3,000 a month. To maintain my investment account, the maximum I can cash out each year is 4%. So as of now I can draw £3,500 per month out of my investment account and still grow my wealth. I could comfortably retire now but I enjoy my work so I'm going to work 3 days a week and then gradually transition into something else."*

Me: *"Will you continue to invest?"*

Salah: *"Absolutely—I will probably never stop investing and pass it all down to my kids!"*

How to Start Investing

Hargreaves Lansdown, Fidelity, Vanguard. These are all companies that offer online investment accounts in the UK. You can create an account, choose your funds and set up a direct debit in 5 minutes. Fees for index funds are generally low, but make sure you compare these before choosing a service. If you are still hesitant, find an accredited financial advisor and tell them what you're trying to achieve.

While Salah chose to invest only in UK stocks, had he put his money into one of the US Index Funds, let's say the S&P 500, he would have around £1.6m in his investment account rather than £1m. American markets have historically performed better than others. Spreading your investments in this way is called *diversification* and in my opinion, is a very balanced approach. If you are interested in this, check in with a financial advisor!

How to Learn More

Millionaire Next Door by Thomas J Stanley, *Intelligent Investor* by Benjamin Graham and *The Lazy Person's Guide to Investing* by Paul Farrell are all great books to get you started with investing. These books excellently summarise and explain the academic evidence behind the approach I've shown you. For further reading, check out *The Essays of Warren Buffet* by

Lawrence Cunningham and *The Little Book of Common Sense Investing* by John Bogle.

How to be Financially Free in 20 Years

I know what you might be thinking: this book is supposed to be about finding and securing a graduate job, why have I just read 10 pages on investing when I don't even have a job?

I went against the advice of my editor and included this chapter to prove that you can still build wealth and achieve financial freedom (FF) without an investment banking salary. Don't invest your time into pursuing high salaried careers if you don't have the necessary skills. You are better off pursuing careers that are meaningful and suited to your skill-set. At the same time, it's difficult to build wealth on a very low salary with limited scope for income growth. So if you do want FF, pick a career that has scope for growth.

Becoming financially free is not reserved for the ultra-intelligent Harvard dropouts. I wanted you to know that. There are plenty of ways to skin a cat and the method I've showed you has been tried and tested across generations. Slow and steady really does win the race.

Secondly, the vast majority of the population never learn about wealth creation. They might occasionally hear a hint from someone who knows what they're doing or have a few semi-serious discussions about index funds and passive income, but they rarely dig into the details and put a financial plan together. Of the ones that do, a fraction actually execute their plan. I wanted to ensure you weren't one of them.

As a best-case scenario, I hope you open a Vanguard account online and deposit £100 of your savings/student loan the moment you finish reading this chapter. I hope you then put £90 in various global index funds and £10 in a global bond index fund.

If you continue to invest like this for the foreseeable future then you could achieve results like Salah.

As a worst-case scenario, I hope that I've planted an idea in your head that makes some sense and piques your interest. At least, enough of an interest to learn more about this topic over time and do the right thing when your first salary payment comes through.

Finally, gradually becoming wealthy over time is easier than taking big risks or breaking your back to earn a high salary. It is less competitive and easier to have a work-life balance. Getting wealthy through investing on a middle-class income is also more sustainable than working 120 hours as a consultant.

To summarise:

1. Expenses are easier to control than earnings. Save by developing good spending habits early.

2. Don't be afraid to negotiate pay increases with your employer. It is a two-way deal.

3. Learn about personal finance and long-term investing by reading books like 'Millionaire Next Door'.

4. Invest in diversified funds and balance your portfolio once a year to ensure it remains in a ratio advised by your financial advisor.

5. Set up a monthly direct debit from your current account to your investment account.

6. Ignore the news, noise and gurus during market crashes.

7. Don't invest your money in opportunities that you don't fully understand or that have insufficient evidence.

8. Contact an accredited financial advisor after you start earning a salary, particularly if you feel hesitant to invest.

Before wrapping up this section of the book, I'm going to teach you're a few lessons about hybrid career paths.

Chapter 14
Hybrid Career Paths

Commission paying, high salary, average salaried jobs and en-trepreneurship—the route to financial freedom isn't limited to only one of these paths. You can work a 9-5 job and then DJ on the weekend for £500 an event. You can work the night-shift and then spend the day picking-up part-time work. You can blog all night, create and sell art or run a business all while working full-time—nothing is stopping you from doing other things.

These are known as hybrid career paths and for some people they are the perfect alternative to regular work.

Peter vs Jane

Peter works 60 hours a week (including commutes) at a pres-tigious firm and earns £60k a year. He works over 3,000 hours a year.

Jane works a total of 35 hours a week (including commutes) and around 1,800 hours a year. She is a nurse for 3 days a week and earns £30k a year. For 4 days a week, she manages her own local 'lip filler' business which contracts 5 of her nursing colleagues. Her booking system is automated online and she only needs to solve the odd problem here or there. This business also earns her £30k a year.

Peter earns £20 an hour and has 39 hours a week of free time; Jane earns £33 an hour and has 53 hours a week of free time.

Who has the better deal? We posed this question to a group of university students, and they responded with the comments in bold below.

Peter is a professional with a prestigious job that commands more social status than a nurse.

Agreed. Peter and everyone around him know that it's much harder to get into his company and do his job. Having that job is like walking around with a permanent badge of honour that provides his ego with a big boost. Except, as I've discussed previously, this isn't necessarily the case. Trust me, freedom trumps social status every day of the week.

Peter might be good at what he does, works with people he loves and makes an altruistic impact.

If this is true, Peter probably has the better deal and his overall life satisfaction will edge ahead of Jane's. However, satisfying all of these areas all at once is very difficult and if you ask most people working in the city which life they would prefer, they would still probably pick Jane's. Don't forget, Jane is a nurse—how's that for impact?

Jane probably had to spend hours setting up the business, arranging contracts with her employees, building the website and app and establishing a customer base

She risked £5000 and about 100 hours of work, until she got her first customer and received her first £50. She won that customer through word of mouth and she has been a regular for years. As for her investment of time and money, she would have spent those 100 hours watching Netflix and spent £5000 on shopping anyway, so she didn't really lose much.

Jane's secondary income is unstable as it's a small business. New competitors could affect her income along with a number of other risks.

There is risk on both sides as Peter could lose his job as well, but it is true that Jane's risk is greater. By choosing a market which is growing and recession proof, her risk of failure drastically reduces. Many people run small businesses all their lives.

Also, while the added risk is a downside for Jane, she has almost unlimited upsides when it comes to earning power. She can choose to work more hours and grow her business if she wants. A business owner is always going to have more potential for substantial income growth than a salaried worker, as there is technically no limit to how big they can grow and how much they can earn.

Ali Webb is a mother of two and founder of Dry Bar, a blow dry business in America. She grew her small blow dry business into a £17m company. How's that for self-actualisation?

Hybrid Career Paths

Carve your own path and don't feel the need to conform to anyone else's template. Being 21 is great, you have your whole life ahead of you and can afford to make some mistakes.

Remember, time is the most valued commodity and money is one of many tools to help you optimise your fulfilment.

Chapter 15
Tangibles (Money)

As discussed in the previous few chapters, the idea that wealth and income are closely related is a fallacy. You can have substantial wealth without having that big of an income, and there are those who have a sizeable income without any real wealth.

If you do want to become financially free as soon as possible, you can do so with pretty much any career path. However, the speed in which you want to obtain financial freedom will depend on the sacrifices you are willing to accept.

High salary jobs, in addition to asking your parents for an early inheritance or starting a business, require an above average level of personal sacrifice, but they can help you achieve financial freedom in 10 years.

Want to be financially free in 20+ years? You can do so sustainably with a middle-class income. There are doctors, police officers, accountants, merchandisers, lawyers, dentists, vets and countless others who have built wealth in this way. In fact, it is estimated that about 10% to 15% of millionaires are in the teaching or education profession. People with stable jobs who can save and invest £500-£1,000 a month for 20-30 years, will become millionaires or even multi-millionaires, if they invest right.

Takeaways from this Section:

1. Your salary can buy you happiness, but only up to £29k in the UK (£39k in London).

2. Aim to achieve financial freedom early or the government will do it for you.

3. Commission based jobs can help you achieve financial freedom (FF) sooner, but only if you have the skill-set to be in the top 10%.

4. High salary jobs can also get you to FF faster, but there is an intangible price to pay (stress & long hours) in exchange for this early boost in income.

5. Working in a regular 9-5, investing and developing good spending habits is a sustainable way to achieve financial freedom in your 30s or 40s (remember Salah).

6. Only a tiny fraction of entrepreneurs achieve the success of those portrayed in the media.

7. Doing a 'side hustle' or working first and then starting a business in the industry you've gained experience in is a safer bet than going knee-deep into a new industry.

How Can you use this Information to Choose the Right Career?

- An ideal near-term target should be to find a job that satisfies all your intangible and tangible needs. Find a meaningful and engaging job that you are good at, that also pays you equal to or an above average salary.

- If a career doesn't satisfy at least 2 of the 3 intangibles (for example, it has meaning and is engaging but you aren't good at it) and won't get you to at least average salary within 3 years, <u>rule it out</u>.

- Look for careers that either tick or have the potential to tick all 3 boxes (MEA) **and** get you to average regional salary levels within 1-3 years.

- From this point, by working hard and smart, you can manoeuvre yourself into a role that gives you more power. You can then pick tasks that are truly meaningful, engaging and that you are good at.

- By spending wisely and investing regularly—such as taking small calculated risks outside of work—you can grow your net worth until you're either partially or fully financially free, all while working in a career that's meaningful and engaging. This will award you with freedom and control to customise your career.

Now that we've got money out of the way, it will be much easier to make calculated career choices. Considering only the tangibles (money) will undeniably result in poor career choices. We have to take a close look at the intangibles too.

Intangibles...

Chapter 16
What you Can't Measure

At the start of this book, I described the three characteristics that make a good career. These were: ability (do something you're good at), meaning (add value to others) and engagement (do something that enables you to reach a state of flow regularly). We're going to dive deeper into these concepts in this section and answer the most common questions I receive from mentees.

How do I assess my skills and figure out what I'm good at now, or what I'll be good at in the future? What do I truly care about, find meaningful and how can I make an impact? What jobs are naturally engaging?

These are hard questions to answer because we're dealing with parts of our personality that we can't measure. When we're dealing with intangible stuff, it helps to put them in buckets. Ask me how much money I have in my bank account, how tall I am, or what my body fat percentage is and I'll be able to give you a fairly definitive answer within a small margin of error. Ask me how good my analytical skills were at university and I'd modestly say, 'Not bad' but in my head, I'd be thinking, 'How long is a piece of string?'. Ask me now and I would confidently say 8/10 relative to the best analysts I know.

We need to put a number on our intangibles but it takes some time and introspection to reduce our margin of error and 'home in' on an accurate figure. We need to assess ourselves like a social scientist assesses happiness—they look at patterns across large data sets and time instead of one-off anecdotal evidence. As philosopher Alain de Botton said, 'We only catch a glimpse or little hints of our tastes. So what we have to do is learn to pick up on their faint sounds.'

In this section of the book, I'm going to show you how to convert these intangibles into tangibles. Although I have drawn from research, much of the advice in this section will be drawn from the field of psychology, my own research and good old common sense.

Chapter 17
Start with What You're Good at

Have you ever sat next to someone in class who was great at solving maths problems or writing essays, and wondered how they were so much better than you? We've all encountered them at some point. Even if you were at the top of your class there's a good chance you knew someone who always seemed to have the edge over you.

They must simply be smarter than you, right? Maybe they have some kind of innate ability they've had since early childhood? Maybe it's down to genetics, or maybe they simply have very intelligent parents who have taught their child from a early age?

I want to introduce you to Shreena:

Me: *"OK – quick-fire round. Letters or numbers?"*

Shreena: *"Letters"*

Genetics clearly play an important role in development and could dictate someone's intelligence. My friend Shreena popped out with a certain set of genetics inherited from her parents that made her slightly more inclined to words than numbers. This didn't necessarily make her an instant wordsmith, but it instilled a proclivity towards words that ensured she developed literacy skills faster than numeracy ones.

At 8 months old, she reached for a book instead of playing with shapes. At school, she achieved better marks in her English test than she did in her maths test. Her English teacher praised her highly and, as a result, she paid more attention to him in class. On family holidays, instead of playing on her phone, Shreena opted for scrabble. She opted for word searches instead of Sudoku. At 16, she had a 20% edge over the rest of her class in 'wordy' subjects like English literature and History. This increased to 25% at 18 and 30% edge at 21.

There are many factors that can influence your intelligence. In Shreena's case, it wasn't a case of "nature or nurture" but rather "nature and *then* nurture".

How you Develop your Speciality

Your brain is more malleable than you realise. Researcher Nathan Fox conducted a study on Romanian orphans that showed how experiences during the first few years of our lives permanently change the structure of our brains.

Up until the 1990s, Romania's orphanages were notorious for being overcrowded, with 40 children to every caregiver. Fox found that children who only spent 6 months or less in these institutions recovered from their neglect quickly and grew up with a 'normal' brain structure. Those who spent longer, however, had far higher rates of social, emotional and cognitive problems during their lives.

We don't need to walk too far to understand how small environmental influences and habits we developed early in our lives can result in significant differences at a later age. You are constantly nudged into activities by parents and siblings. From the toys you reach for and the TV programs you choose to the conversations you have around the dinner table; all of these day-to-day activities shape your aptitude. This is another example of *gradualism.*

This knowledge, aptitude and cognitive ability compound over time like compound interest. Shreena started her first day at school with a 4% edge over her peers in English Language. Her teachers noticed this, gave her more praise and harder work. This feedback loop continued throughout her entire education and as a result, she walked into university with a 30% edge over her peers in written communication.

When people asked Shreena how she became so good at writing, her answers were fairly generic and modest. She would tell them it was all down to practice or hard work, or insist that she simply had good teachers. Deep down she couldn't pinpoint the exact reason, because the reality is that there were multiple reasons that all combined to create the person she became. The real explanation would have gone something like this:

"I was born with a slightly above-average aptitude towards words which gradually compounded over time through the actions of my parents, siblings and teachers. The 80%+ marks you see me get now are a result of 19 years of compounding."

Like Shreena, you had very little control over your 'genetic edge' or the level of compounding you received growing up, particularly in the first 8-10 years of your life. This means people are going to be better than you at certain tasks. However, you also have skills which are far more advanced than your peers and those in your age group. It's very easy to ignore or forget this because we have a nasty habit of obsessing over our shortcomings.

Just because you aren't a maths Olympiad or a grand master chess player, doesn't mean all hope is lost. You have an edge somewhere. Whether this is a big or small edge is irrelevant because as long as you develop good habits then you have plenty of time to continue compounding.

With enough data points, you'll eventually identify your circle of competence and learn that staying inside of it benefits you in many ways; both tangible and intangible.

What if you Know what your Compounded Aptitude is?

If you have a glaringly obvious aptitude towards a particular skill or set of skills, that matters. It matters a lot. Don't ignore it. It's probably the most important data point or 'edge' you have when it comes to choosing a career. It's surprising how many people disregard their own 'talents'.

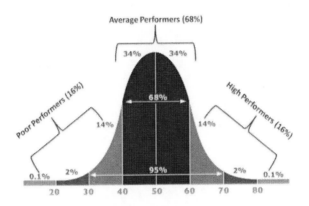

One guy I knew from high school was very good with numbers. His mental maths was incredibly fast. He won regional maths championships and was most certainly somewhere on the right-hand side of the performance bell curve when it came to numbers. Then he went for Optometry. What?! Frustratingly, he had awesome grades and his first choice was a mid-level university that specialised in Optometry.

His choice confused the hell out of me at the time, but I later learned that he secured a position in quantitative finance at a hedge fund. Whether he enjoyed this job or felt a sense of fulfilment from it is a whole other conversation. Usually, these jobs pay six-figures a few years out of university. From a purely monetary perspective he would have been in a great position to achieve financial freedom by the age of 30.

The moral of the story is that if you have awards sitting on a shelf and hundreds of people have paid you compliments over certain abilities that you possess, take note. These compounded aptitudes should be at the centre of all your career discussions.

Most people, including myself, don't have a glaringly obvious outlier skill or aptitude. When I was 18 there were no awards for maths, writing, art, debating, public speaking, sports or engineering sitting on my shelf. I didn't even have a shelf. Not all of us can be the best in any one area, but we can be exceptional in our combinations.

Combinations

Let's imagine that you're an average writer with a good sense of humour. Becoming a successful author or journalist would be a bit of a stretch and the same could be said for stand-up comedy. However, you could combine these skills to become an excellent comedy writer. You could write comedy articles, jokes—you could even learn scriptwriting and start penning scripts for TV or film.

The vast majority of successful people are rarely defined by a single skill. They fuse their skills, and while some of these skills are far from exceptional, they combine to create something that is truly extraordinary. Steve Jobs was not the world's greatest designer, engineer or businessman, for instance, but he did have a unique approach to all of these things, and wove them together into something outstanding.

If you don't have one major outlier skill, take a holistic view of your smaller skills and combine them into something more valuable.

If someone looked at all my core skills and graded them against the 800,000 other 18 year olds in the country, most of them would be in the 40-70% range of the bell curve. Taking the time to figure out which of my skills were closer to the 70% part of the bell curve ultimately helped me find the best combination and make the correct career choices. I call these 'outlier skills', and the best way to identify them is by creating a 'skills-stack sheet'. I'm going to show you how to build your own.

Skills-Stack Sheet

We'll build this framework in an Excel spreadsheet that you should update every 6 months over the next 3 years as you manoeuvre yourself onto your most optimum career path. Ideally, you should keep this sheet for the rest of your life. I have a folder on my computer where I keep various information for my eyes only. It contains my own skills-stack sheet. I suggest you keep one too.

In this Excel sheet, we are going to break down your skills into i-skills and c-skills. I've outlined what these are in *How to ACE Your Degree* and *How to be Admired & Respected*, but in case you haven't read these books I'll summarise now.

i-skills is short for Introvert-Skills. These are the skills you use when you are working on your own and they include:

1. Numeracy
2. Language
3. Creative (Images & Audio)

c-skills is short for Charisma-Skills. These are skills used when interacting with other people and include:

1. Verbal communication
2. Emotional intelligence and empathy
3. Influence and persuasion

We will then break these 6 skills down further into 'granular skills' that you need to identify and score using:

1. Introspection (thinking about yourself a lot)
2. Qualitative research (asking other people to think about you a lot)
3. Psychometric and aptitude tests

In an ideal world, we are well-rounded individuals who achieve top grades and develop a high-level of social intelligence in equal proportions. In reality, our skills compound at different rates and most of us end up stronger in one more than the other.

For example, I know with certainty that my i-skills are stronger than my c-skills. Someone who had a conversation with me or watched my TEDx talk wouldn't be able to tell, because I've worked hard to develop both. However, I can and so can those who are very close to me. In fact, I'm able to discuss my strengths in much more detail than most people because I've kept a 'skills stack sheet' since university. You'll see what it looks like on the next page.

Core	Score	Evidence	Granular skills	Score	Evidence
Numbers	7	Numerical reasoning test: 70% average	Problem solving	8	Higher marks in 'short answer' maths calculations at GCSE (A), A-level (A) and Uni (AAA) -
			Analysis	8	Maths and Physics coursework at A-Level (A) and Uni (72%)
			Accounting/Excel	7	Projects requiring extensive excel work have received high marks from GCSE (A) to Uni (72% 69%). Internship examples too (4/5 in feedback review)
			Mental maths	5	Can only do single digit addition, subtracting and multiplication quickly - only half of practice interview Qs answered correctly
Language	6	Verbal reasoning test: 60% average	Comprehension	6	May need to read text more than once to fully understand - english comprehension and written prose subjects grades. English GCSE (C)
			Explaining	8	Good at explaining detailed procedures - GCSE ICT (A), procedure project during internship & process engineering grade of 80%+
			Grammer/Spelling	4	Rely on spell check and grammerly
			Opinion/Analysis	4	60% average across essay based subjects at uni
Creative	6	Explorer Activity Manager - 2nd in Group	Video editing	7	Travel and animation videos - good feedback on social media and from media manager
			Filming	7	High score in explorer activity film project (Came 2nd in group)
			Creative writing	5	High score in script writing but overall poor creative writing scores throughout school (C - B)
			Programming	7	Basic programming on easy language - good feedback
Other			Critical thinking	8	Able to rationally evaluate problems and see connections between ideas - lab marks at uni above 75% and A-level work (A)
			Time management	6	Half of coursework from previous year left to last minute and had to do all nighters
			Delayed gratification	9	Friends/family have often said that I 'Never give up' - 'Always persevere' and have a lot of 'self-discipline'
			Organisation	6	Feedback from tutor and general observation over the years. Room/common areas often a little untidy but OK compared to others

i-Skills

158

How to Land Your Dream Graduate Job

c-skills

Core	Score	Evidence	Granular skills	Score	Evidence
Verbal Communication	7	Presentation Marks	Oral articulation	6	Muble and stutter more than most when unprepared (internship - manager feedback)
			Public speaking	7	Good presentation marks and feedback - (73%). Family public speaking event - feedback
			Debate	5	Tend to avoid conflict and debate as not confident in positioning arguments clearly off the cuff
			Communication	7	Can explain complex information when prepared - struggle when unprepared - internship feedback (3/5)
Emotional Intelligence & Empathy	5	Friends & Family Feedback	Conflict management	6	2 strong examples of resisting high pressure and verbal attacks. Several compliments over the years
			Difficult people	5	Design project and Jao - Ali
			Passive people	7	Design project Jenna
			Advice	8	Several compliments from younger people/mentees saying that I give well thought out advice
Influence & Persuasion	6	Conversion Rate of Interviews	Humour	6	Niche humour, but generally described as funny on most social groups - not usually the funniest though
			Sales	6	Never really had to sell much or taken on selling part time jobs. No compliments or feedback
			Reading others	5	Described as emotionally inept at times!
			Leadership	6	Not afraid to take hold of leadership position
Other			Patience	8	Word often used to describe me
			Temperment	8	Rarely get angry and/or judge others - got it from mum
			Confidence	7	Tend to put my hand up or put myself forward more than others.

Start with What You're Good at

I-Skills and C-Skills

How does a recruiter evaluate you? They first combine your psychometric test scores with your academic qualifications to give you a score, which they then compare with your peer group. This is essentially a valuation of your i-skills. If you achieve a high score, they invite you for several rounds of assessments which usually consist of face-to-face interviews and assessment centres. Some companies put you through team exercises, as well as panel and case study interviews. These are all designed to test your c-skills.

Much of the way we evaluate ourselves should be more or less the same as how a recruiter values us, allowing us to see where our strengths lie. We also need to be 100% honest with our inner recruiter and not let our ego massage the figures.

As you can see from my skills stack sheet, there are 3 core skills for both i and c-skills. These are broken down into 'granular skills'. Every skill is given a score out of 10 with one or more pieces of evidence to justify that score. For example:

Core	Score	Evidence	Granualar skills	Score	Evidence
Numbers	7	Numerical reasoning test: 70% average	Problem solving	8	Higher marks in 'short answer' maths calculations at GCSE (A), A-level (A) and Uni (AAA)
			Analysis	8	Maths and Physics coursework at A-Level (A) and Uni (72%)
			Accounting/ Excel	7	Projects requiring extensive excel work have received high marks from GCSE (A) to Uni (72% 69%). Internship examples too (4/5 in feedback review)
			Mental maths	5	Can only do single digit addition, subtracting and multiplication quickly - only half of practice interview Qs answered correctly

My numeracy skills were scored at 7, and I based this on my numerical reasoning scores. I then noted granular skills that involved numbers, brainstormed pieces of evidence from the past and gave myself a score.

I know that scoring yourself out of 10 for various skills isn't the most exact science, but it's good enough for the purpose it serves. Laying your aptitudes out like this gets you thinking about what you're really good at. It forces you to trawl through your past for clues and keep your eyes peeled in the future for data points. You're going to have to trust me on this one—take a leap of faith, create a sheet of your own and update it once a year for the next 3-4 years at least. You'll thank me later.

How to Score your Core I-Skills

The majority of people only look at practice psychometric tests when provided one by an employer. If you are serious about making the right career choice, you should complete practical numerical and verbal reasoning tests the moment you finish this chapter.

Psychometric companies have invested a lot of money into ensuring the results from their tests accurately represent the core skills of individuals. Big companies place a lot of weight on them and, if you ask most HR staff, they work well.

At the time of writing, most employers get their tests from a company called SHL. You can visit this company's website at shldirect.com, where you'll find both tests. Once you've completed these tests, round your final marks up to the nearest whole number and enter these into your skills-stack sheet. For example, if you achieved numerical and verbal reasoning scores of 63% and 76% respectively, enter 6 and 8 in the excel sheet.

Your creative score will be based on your ability to innovate and exercise creative talents. These can be art, music composition, photography, videography or creative writing. If you have any experience in these or other creative skills, enter them under the granular column of your sheet and score them first, before taking an average of these to give yourself an overall score. For example, if you scored a 6 for photography and 4 for creative writing, your core creative score should be 5 $((6 + 4)/2)$.

How to Score your Granular I-Skills

I-skills are easier to score then c-skills because we've been in academia all our lives and have been assessed rigorously over the past 5-6 years. Your exam results don't determine whether you will be successful or not in life, but they do hold very tangible clues about you and your aptitudes.

We are all graded on a curve. If you achieved an A* in English Language at GCSE, that means you performed better than 90% of the 600,000 others who also took the exam. Does this mean you have an edge in written communication? Most likely. Other factors, such as the quality of your school or the competence of your teacher, play a much smaller role compared to your compounded aptitude.

You want to see consistency across your exam results over the past few years. If you have a B in maths GCSE; A in maths A-level and A's in maths modules at university, score yourself a 7.

Did you achieve an A* in your maths GCSE a year early and then got top marks at A-level maths, followed by bronze in the maths Olympiad? It's safe to say that you're a level 8 or 9 numerical problem solver.

If you received an A* in GCSE maths and haven't touched the subject since, your numerical problem-solving score should still be above a 6. 2-3 years doesn't wipe out your core numeracy skills.

What's 37 x 24? If you got the answer in less than 7 seconds, put yourself down for an 8 or above for mental maths.

Dig out some old report cards from school and college, are there any common themes or phrases used to describe any of the skills you possess?

What did you get in your SATS?

What subjects did you choose at GCSE and what were your final grades?

What subjects did you choose at 6th form and what were your final grades?

What about the modules you picked at university?

What have friends, parents and teachers complimented you on in the past?

Take a moment to word-vomit 500 words onto a word processor to try and identify your granular skills. Think back over your school years when you surprised yourself with a grade.

During GCSE ICT, I was tasked with finishing a project on how to build pivot tables in Excel. After completing the work fairly quickly and with little fuss, I achieved the highest mark in my class three times. This never happened in any of my other subjects. Was this an outlier skill associated with process and written communication? Absolutely.

During my internship at Goldman Sachs, I had to complete written procedures for various ad-hoc tasks completed by my team. I nailed it and my manager highlighted this twice in my appraisals. This was yet another data point which showed that I had a compounded aptitude for processes and written communication.

When I began my graduate job, I manoeuvred myself into an algorithmic trader position because my process driven skills lend themselves well to computer programming.

I'm good at giving step-by-by step instructions for complex tasks and have an aptitude for written communication, specifically non-fiction. On the back of this, I decided to write my first book, *How to ACE Your A-Levels*.

This is why my books have sold so well. Countless students have complimented my ability to simplify and explain how people should achieve top grades.

How to Score your Granular C-Skills

It is much harder to measure your c-skills than it is your i-skills. As I mentioned in *How to be Admired & Respected*, an interview by a top company is to c-skills what an A-level exam is to i-skills. Set up a few practice interviews with your university careers centre and ask for feedback, with questions like:

On a scale of 1-10, how was my:

1. Oral articulation
2. Persuasiveness
3. Ability to explain and describe
4. Listening skills
5. Eye contact
6. Posture
7. Overall verbal communication

Think of past experiences where you've had to exercise your c-skills. When you last spoke in front of a large group of people, did you project your voice with authority? Have you ever had a client facing part-time job as a sales assistant or barista? If so, what kind of feedback did your manager give on the way you interacted with others? Did he/she criticise or praise you for anything in particular?

Trawl through your past and write 500 words on as many past experiences you can think of. Use this qualitative introspection, in combination with feedback from your interview, to identify granular c-skills and score them as honestly as possible.

Myers Briggs

There are many different aptitude tests on the market right now. My personal favourite, and the one that most experts prefer, is the Myers Briggs personality test. Developed by psychologists and mother-daughter team Katherine Cook Briggs and Isabel Briggs Myers, this test is used by thousands of top companies around the world.

There is a wealth of data on Myers Briggs personality profiles and their compatibility with regards to certain careers. This is something mildly tangible that we can hold on to and use to make career decisions. As you dig into the research, you'll find some useful facts. For example, my profile type is INTP and we are in the minority. Only 3% of the population are INTPs as opposed to ESTJs and ESTPs, which both make up 10%.

Tests conducted at technology firms in Silicon Valley show that over 40% of employees are INTPs. Coincidence? Unlikely. Is it safe to assume that software programming is a well-suited career path for someone like me? Almost certainly.

Take one of the free Myers Briggs tests online and note down your personality type. Read through the description for your personality type on mbtionline.com and note down any common themes between this and your earlier introspective research. Enter this data into the evidence columns in your skills framework if necessary.

Start with what you're good at

After you complete your research and skills-stack sheet, close your laptop, revisit it the following day and highlight the top 3-5 skills that really stand out.

Once you've done this, it's time to filter those key phrases down to a single paragraph pitch which you can use during the graduate recruitment process. Do you see where we are going with this? Not only will this sheet help you decide what you want to do, but it will outline your skill-set to potential employers and ensure you standout from the competition. Knowing what you're good at is not enough, you need to be able to articulate it clearly and back it up with evidence.

Doing all of the above and continuously updating your skills framework will put you in an unbelievably good position by the time you hit 23. We'll discuss this further in the 'Decisions, Decisions…' section of the book.

Chapter 18
How to Find Engaging Work

My dad was obsessed with taking pictures when I was younger. He was an aspiring Instagrammer during the dawn of the digital age. He took his camera everywhere with him, snapping pictures of friends, family, and anything else that caught his eye. He would then get these pictures printed and hand them out as gifts

Noting wrong with that, right?

The problem is, he would do this completely unannounced, rocking-up to their homes out of the blue with nothing but a smile and a photograph they didn't even realise had been taken.

To the relief of his busy friends, many of which had young children to care for and complicated lives to juggle, he stopped rocking up to the front door after I taught him how to use e-mail.

Photography had been a big part of my dad's life and I had seen firsthand how much joy it had given him, so as I grew I naturally began to reach for the camera myself. He would buy the latest gadgets, from digital cameras to photo printers and smartphones, and then insist that I teach him how to use them, so I gradually became just as obsessed as he was.

When on holiday, I kept an eye out for interesting people or wildlife to record and looked forward to getting home quickly to see what I'd come up with. As soon as I had something worthwhile, I'd sprint into the house, setup my equipment, and then piece together a reel of all the footage I'd taken.

Long periods of time went by where I didn't touch a camera or video editing software, but I somehow kept coming back to this hobby. I created an Instagram account @boygirltravels just for fun and grew to a few thousand followers with minimal effort.

People often ask me, 'Isn't it cumbersome to take all this footage all the time, organise it and edit it?'. It can take a lot of time, but it doesn't feel like work to me. I actually enjoy recording my trips abroad more than the trip itself.

My affinity towards video and photo content creation isn't a passion. As I mentioned earlier, passion is short-lived and usually led by a vision or fantasy of the future. I don't daydream about becoming a wildlife photographer.

This is an activity that I *intrinsically enjoy* because of mental models that I'd developed from a young age when my brain was at its most malleable. It's unlikely that these models will change as I age.

How Identifying what you Enjoy can Help you Choose an Engaging Career

When I launched my business, I had to do various business functions on my own—legal, accounting, product development (writing), inbound marketing, outbound sales. After asking my business mentor and partner to provide feedback on my skills, he gave the following scores:

Legal – C
Accounting – A
Product development – A
Marketing – A*
Sales – B

If we looked deeper into marketing:

Video animation – A*
Image campaigns – A
e-mail campaigns – B
Digital campaign creating & management – A
Data analysis – A
Social media management – A
TEDx talk – B

Some people spend tens of thousands of pounds creating video content for their marketing campaigns. I achieved over 4,000,000 views across all my campaign videos using £12 a month animation software and I had a blast doing it. Hours

171

would go by as I created marketing scripts and voice recordings and iterated the video animations to perfection. Animation videos are different from the live footage and editing I did as a kid, but there are enough similar characteristics for me to enjoy the work.

Every time I uploaded a new video, I felt like a 10-year-old again, excited to see what people thought of my creation. I'd check the view count obsessively and trawl through the analytics on viewer engagement and drop-off rates. If I was to ever go back into employment, one of my options would most certainly be video content creation and digital marketing.

When analysing the history behind successful high-impact entrepreneurs, there is almost always some evidence that intrinsic enjoyment played a part in their career decisions. Adam D'Angelo, ex CTO of Facebook and founder of Quora, competed in TopCoder coding competitions for fun. Countless athletes started playing their respective sports at a young age.

What Engages you?

What tasks capture your attention to the point that you lose track of time? What do you do on a Sunday? How do you absorb content—reading, audio or video? Did you doodle and draw on your workbooks growing up? Did you complete a lot of word searches or Sudoku? These are all clues to find tasks you intrinsically enjoy.

If you prefer watching videos over reading, then working in video marketing as opposed to copy marketing may be the best bet. When you intrinsically enjoy a task, time flies like you're on auto-pilot. Usually, people have a reasonably good instinct when it comes to tasks they enjoy and can climb the corporate ladder quicker, because their skills will naturally increase faster doing something they love.

If you can identify tasks that you intrinsically enjoy, make a small textbox in the bottom right corner of your self-stack sheet and list them.

Chapter 19

How to Find Meaningful Work

According to a survey by PayScale, these are the most meaningful jobs:

1. Clergy (98% of employees find their job meaningful)
2. English Language & Literature Teachers, Postsecondary (96%)
3. Directors, Religious Activities & Education (96%)
4. Surgeons (96%)
5. Education Administrators, Elementary & Secondary School (95%)
6. Radiation Therapists (93%)
7. Chiropractors (92%)
8. Psychiatrists (92%)
9. Anaesthesiologists (91%)
10. Rehabilitation Counsellors (91%)
11. Occupational Therapists (91%)
12. Primary School Teachers (91%)
13. Epidemiologists (91%)

The least meaningful jobs are:

1. Car park attendant (5% consider their job meaningful)
2. Gaming supervisor (20%)
3. Prepress technician (25%)
4. Title examiner, abstractor and searcher (25%)
5. Fabric and apparel patternmaker (25%)
6. Welding, soldering and brazing machine operators (26%)
7. Counter and rental clerks (26%)
8. Crushing, grinding and polishing machine operators (26%)
9. Purchasing agents and buyers, farm products (26%)
10. Fashion designers (26%)

Gaming supervisors are those who work on casino floors, like blackjack dealers. Some may tell themselves that they are helping people unwind and have a good time, but deep down, they know most of the people that sit at their table are going to lose money over the long-term. Most gaming staff understand that they take more value from their customers than they add. It's no surprise that only 20% of them feel their job is meaningful.

In the group of the most meaningful jobs, most are related to medicine and education. What does that tell us? Meaningful work involves helping other people in some shape or form. The top 12 professions of this group are only one degree of separation away from those they are helping.

A surgeon can see the value they are adding to an individual and their families with their own eyes. Teachers interact with their students on a daily basis and receive a dopamine hit every time their students have a eureka moment. These are what I call 'direct impact' jobs.

Direct Impact

Medicine and education consistently provide meaningful careers. This is one of the reasons university courses related to medicine receive the highest number of applications each year. Of the 1.8m UK university places on offer in 2018/2019, 254,000 applications were for subjects related to medicine. People instinctively know that a job that directly helps people is going to make them feel good.

Medics tend to earn more than education professionals, thereby improving their ability to control their career and optimise job satisfaction. It takes a lot of time and effort to become a consultant, but once you're there, financial freedom can be achieved in a few short years and an array of options will be available to you.

If you have outlier skills or a combination of skills that suit a job in medicine or education, pull the trigger! If you have no interest in these areas and don't have suited skills, what should you do? What if you are helping people from a distance? Can you find meaning in 'indirect impact' jobs?

Indirect Impact

The world has many important problems that need solving, and they vary in size and significance. Climate change, poverty and disease are the top 3 in my opinion because they are current problems that pose a significant threat to the human race. Countless government and non-profits are focused on all three areas. The largest philanthropic trust in the world, the Bill & Malinda Gates Foundation, has focused its efforts on the latter two.

Other potential problems that could cause large scale global catastrophe include hostile artificial intelligence, nuclear holocaust, bioterrorism, cyberterrorism, natural pandemics, destructive biotechnology or nanotechnology and global war.

Epidemiologists are scientists who study diseases. They analyse what causes disease outbreaks in order to treat existing diseases and prevent future outbreaks. Their efforts could potentially impact millions of people's lives, but they are silent heroes.

Millions won't be lining up outside their doors, lovingly embracing them and thanking them for saving their lives. Would this job be as meaningful and satisfying as a surgeon's? 91% of Epidemiologists do find their job meaningful, so potentially yes, but it is entirely dependent on the individual.

Does helping 100 people provide more meaning than helping 1? Absolutely. What if you don't know any of those 100 people and that 1 person is your mother? Positively impacting your mum's life is obviously going to mean more to you. Following that same logic, what if the 100 people were random and you could relate to that 1 person in a very meaningful way?

Let's say your brother has Down's syndrome and you have the option to work for two production companies. One is a huge Hollywood studio and the other a small production company that creates videos to help special needs kids learn Makaton or sign language. You're probably going to find more meaning in the latter.

This may be the reason why the Clergy tops the list when it comes to meaning. They are continuously helping people in their community. The first step is to identify what you currently find meaningful or what you could potentially find meaningful.

What do I Find Meaningful?

There is no objective standard to measure meaning. In asking a question like this, *you* have set the standard, *you* have set the measure, and *you* are doing the testing! Such estimation of yourself can take place inside or outside of your awareness. To determine what you might find meaningful, it's worth looking at events in your past.

Let me tell you a story.

Sitting in the living room chatting with two of my best friends, Dinesh and Kav, and their mum, Harsha, I heard the front door open and close. Their dad, Suraj, walked in after a long flight from California. He entered the living room, sat down and didn't greet anyone. Even as a quiet man, this was unusual as he would usually give us all a big smile and say something. We all carried on our conversation and didn't think anything of it.

Ten minutes later, with his head stiffly facing straight ahead and his hands on his lap, Suraj moved his eyes to his right then back again. He did it again a minute later, then again and again. At this point, his eyes were rapidly moving back and forth. We all knew something was horribly wrong, and Harsha started screaming as she tried to get him stop.

Suddenly, Suraj's eyes rolled back and his body began shaking uncontrollably. He was having a stroke. Dinesh called the ambulance, and we all helped administer first aid and cleared the pathway for the paramedics. During those ten minutes, I saw both my friends experience a rollercoaster of emotions. They were pacing up and down the house trying to hide their tears from me. Thankfully, the paramedics arrived promptly and he survived.

For most of Dinesh and Kav's lives up until that point, their biggest concerns were talking to girls and convincing their parents to buy the next Grand Theft Auto. Life was normal, until it wasn't. Within the space of fifteen minutes, they went from worrying about having to go to bed early to worrying if their dad was going to survive. Dinesh and Kav were in their early teens when they saw all this, and it left a very large emotional scar.

When it came time to apply to university, unsurprisingly, both of them chose medicine. Consciously or not, they saw meaning in that profession. Trauma can be horrible at the time, but it can also redefine the way in which you see the world and what you find meaningful. One is now on an accelerated programme to become a surgeon and the other is a psychiatrist. Both love their jobs.

How to Find Meaningful Work

To find meaningful work, look no further than careers that help others directly and indirectly. To find work that is meaningful **to you**, find work that helps people you care about or relate to.

Chapter 20
Intangibles

Of all the intangibles we have spoken about so far, your skills are the most important. It's possible to be happy in your job even if you aren't good at it, but your lack of accomplishment will upset you eventually. You will also be reducing your earning potential and ability to achieve financial freedom earlier. No matter what anyone says, you have a set of outlier-skills that can be combined to produce magic. Keep an eye out for them!

Meaning comes next. This is an easier box to tick and it helps you narrow down your options. Your past can provide clues as to what you truly care about.

You may not be able to secure a career that is meaningful to you straight out of university and may need to gain more experience first. This is common, particularly for non-medics, and there is nothing wrong with pursuing careers that are a good personal fit for a few years. The job market isn't going anywhere and new opportunities will arise eventually.

If your work has meaning to you and you are good at it, you are 70% there. Over time, by building relationships and performing well, you can customise your career and take on more engaging day-to-day tasks.

The top takeaways from this section are:

1. When choosing a career path, your outlier skills and combinations matter the most.

2. Create a skills framework and update it once a year for the next few years.

3. Use introspection, qualitative research and aptitude tests to score yourself.

4. Tasks that engage you are often those you've had exposure to in your childhood.

5. Don't let social status and the allure of big brands influence your decision making. Ability, engagement and meaning are more important.

Armed with a skills-stack sheet, you can now start looking for jobs.

Intangibles

Skills:
- YOU: Outlier and combinations.
- JOB: Required skills/day to day tasks.

Meaning:
- YOU: Emotional trauma and/or triumph during childhood.
- JOB: Jobs that help others, high impact (more people the better).

Engagement:
- YOU: Tasks that engaged you in the past, hobbies, what you do on a Sunday.
- JOB: Jobs that have Autonomy, Feedback, etc.,

Tangibles

- We are looking at jobs that can help us achieve financial freedom before our retirement age.

After discovering what your outlier skills and combinations are, look for companies that help people you can relate to.

The Ultimate Career Strategy…

Chapter 21
Iterate your Way Towards an Ideal Career

Prior to writing this book, I contacted several of my friends and university and asked them some questions relating to their approach to job hunting. Here's what I found:

61% of my sample set started 'properly' focusing on jobs in their final year of university, missing all internship opportunities.

When I asked why they didn't start sooner, the most common answer was:

"I had a lot of work at university".

Closely followed by:

"I thought I'd get most of my degree work out the way first and then focus properly on jobs".

and:

"I didn't really know what I wanted to do".

Clearly, the demands of university and indecision stop people from making progress.

32% never went to see a careers advisor.

People tend to ask for careers advice from their family and friends, which is OK. However, there are people out there who are trained to help you identify your outlier skills by asking the right questions.

71% said the people around them influenced their career decisions.

One of the reasons I started applying early, relative to the rest of my year group, was because I had a lot of friends studying Maths and Economics. Most of them were interested in accounting, consulting, actuary and investment banking jobs. Competition in these industries was much higher than engineering. As a result, my maths friends started looking at internships halfway through university and when I took the job race seriously, my closest friends followed suit. The culture of your year group and your closest friends will have a big influence on your decisions.

89% regretted not starting earlier and ended up 'panic applying'.

If no one around you is taking career hunting seriously and university is piling on the work, you will miss critical internship deadlines and may end up 'panic applying' in your final year.

If you don't know what you want to do, narrowing down your options will take time. It may take several months of research and introspection, if you want to do it properly. Those who leave this research to the last-minute end up skipping this step entirely. They then focus on finding **any** job rather than the **right** job.

I have spoken to over 300 undergraduates and surveyed many more. I've learned that those who failed used indecision as an excuse to not take action—they were afraid of the unfamiliar terrain that followed almost two decades of education.

This section of the book will show you that finding your ideal career is an iterative process where failure is not only normal, but necessary.

Pick-Aim-Fire-Check (PAFC)

Your goal shouldn't be to find *any* job, it should be to identify a career that will bring consistent and sustainable satisfaction into your life. This is what the PAFC approach will help you achieve.

Picture yourself standing in front of a massive board which has every single profession available to you. All professions are grouped into 3 columns: Words, Numbers and Creative.

Words	Numbers	Creative

intro

extro

Within the extro area of the graph, you have jobs that are heavily focused on people skills. These include jobs that require relationship management like Equity Derivatives Sales and Client Relationship Management. Under i-skills, you have software development and copywriting. Within the 'creative' section you have jobs that mainly require spatial intelligence and diagrammatical reasoning. These include architecture, animation and graphic design.

In front of you are two guns:

How to Land Your Dream Graduate Job

1. Shotgun
2. Sniper rifle

When you fire a shotgun, the bullets spread out, impacting a large area. A sniper rifle, on the other hand, is more focused and impacts a smaller area.

Your job over the next few years is to find the most suitable profession by shooting the board in the right areas. Hitting an outlier skill will achieve a higher number of points. You have a limited number of shots. What strategy would you use to achieve the highest number of points?

Step 1 – PICK – Choose your Weapon

What gun you choose largely depends on your conviction in a particular career path, as well as the richness of your skills-stack sheet and how close you are to internship and graduate deadlines.

Which one of these groups are you in?

1. I know exactly what I want to do. I'm going for a high-barrier to entry job.

2. I'm probably going to do something related to my degree but am open to looking at other industries.

3. I don't have a clue what to do.

If you are in group 1, you are sniper and I'm not going to stand in your way. If you're hellbent on a particular career path and have been for several years, then go 'all in'. One in ten students I come across are in this group and I can usually see their passion within the first 30 seconds of speaking with them.

Alex, a guy I knew at college was obsessed with becoming a doctor from the age of 16. He didn't get the grades, so he went for a Biomedical Sciences course with the intention to move on to medicine later. Alex got a 2:1 in that degree but still struggled to get into medical school. At this point I thought he'd change his mind and try something else, but he didn't. He took a £20k loan out, travelled to a Polish university and studied an additional 5 years to get his qualification! When I asked him if it was all worth it, he said:

"Yes and no. Being a doctor is great, but I'm in so much debt and am several years behind everyone. I had to do it though. I've wanted it ever since I was a kid and would have wondered 'what if?' my whole life if I didn't try. Overall, I'm happy with the decision".

When my mentees ask me whether they should change their degree course during an existential crisis, nine times out of ten I advise them to stay put and focus on job hunting. Only when I encounter an individual like Alex, someone obsessed with a particular career path for many years. do I change my tune. It's not worth living a life with that much regret, and if you want something that badly, you owe it to yourself to try.

If you are in group 1, and you know if you are, it's still worth reading through this section of the book. However, if you really don't feel it applies to you, feel free to skip over to the 'Fire' section. For those in group 2 and 3, I'm going to run through a tried and trusted strategy that will help you find and secure the perfect career.

If you've never had a real job and are still a teenager, starting with the shotgun strategy makes sense as you can impact a large area of the board and have a greater chance of understanding your most suitable opportunities. Starting your own business, working for small companies and firm-wide rotation schemes at medium-large size companies are examples of 'shotgun strategies'.

This is where your skills-stack sheet comes in handy. If your scores are quite similar and you can't identify any outlier skills, then you don't know enough about yourself to aim anywhere on the board. Starting your own business would be the best option and I'll explain why later.

By using a shotgun strategy, you will gain exposure to many different types of work and exercise both your i & c-skills. Many of my mentees who used this strategy uncovered areas of work that they were good at but never considered before. This isn't really that surprising. How are you supposed to know what you are truly good at and find engaging unless you try it?

There are accountants out there who would be excellent marketers and dentists who are well suited to sales. Unfortunately, our system encourages us to specialise very early. Wouldn't it be great if we could spend time working in a large variety of professions before taking a leap? This is exactly what a shotgun strategy helps you do.

Already had some work experience and a healthy-skills stack sheet? Then you should know what your outlier skills are. Pick up the sniper rifle and focus on a particular area or specialisation.

Step 2 – AIM – Where should you aim first?

Now we use your skills-stack sheet to help us narrow down your career options. If you have a clear outlier skill, then you should aim towards careers that require that skill.

Let's say your c-skills score is 7/10 and i-skills is 5/10. You should be aiming towards careers that require better than average c-skills. Within your c-skills, if persuasion and 'negotiation' are key phrases that are highlighted, you can narrow down your options even further.

What industries are c-skills oriented? All professions require a good level of interpersonal skills but some more than others.

Media & entertainment, hospitality and consulting spring to mind. Career advisors can help you in this stage. It's at this point, you need to start putting together *career-stack sheets* to help us compare and objectively choose what to prioritise. I'll show you how to do this in chapter 24.

Step 3 – FIRE – Pull the Trigger

After you've picked your career path(s), it's all about efficient execution. Many undergrads spend far too long tweaking their CVs and fine-tuning their application answers—just get it done and don't fuss over the details. Securing interviews for internships, short-term work placements and graduate jobs is a numbers game.

Psychometric tests, phone/face-to-face interviews and assessment centres come next. Social skills are of utmost importance here and completing the 6-month charisma project described in *How to be Admired & Respected*, will give you an edge. Being judged by intimidating 50 year olds will be uncomfortable at first but you will get used to it and eventually start enjoying the experience. I'll run you through my approach to execution towards the tail end of this book.

Step 4 – CHECK – What Did you Learn?

After each work placement, it's imperative that you receive frank and honest feedback from those you worked with. This can be painful, but it's essential and will help you in the long run. I received horrible feedback from one of my managers and it crushed my ego, but in hindsight it was a useful experience that I learned a lot from.

Were there any tasks that your manager or team members thought you performed well in? What skills did you exercise during those tasks and why did you perform well in them? Are there any commonalities with those tasks and similar ones you've done elsewhere? Did you find any of the work particularly engaging? Analyse your experience, update your skills-stack sheet and go back to Step 1.

Iterating your Way Towards an Ideal Career

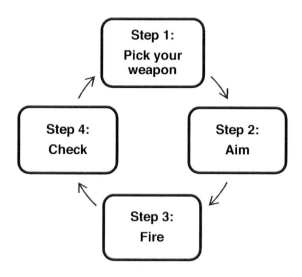

PAFC is the best way to focus on your ideal career as it runs simulations for skill-suitability. There is only so much theory and psychometric testing you can do. You will need to get out into the field, become very efficient at securing work experience and objectively evaluate how you perform every time you enter a work place.

It's messy and emotionally draining at first, but you'll get used to it. Humans are emotional creatures, no matter how daunting or tiring a particular process is, we always adapt. Towards the end of university, I'd walk into interviews with maximum confidence and leave with very little concern over whether I got the job or not. If it was a no, it would sting a little but I'd get over it quickly and would then focus on the next one. Only when I took this stoic approach did I start making final rounds consistently and eventually got offers on the table.

From starting your own business to graduate jobs, over the next few chapters I'm going to describe the best shotgun and sniper strategies (Step 1). I'll then show you how to use your stack sheet to help narrow down your options and aim for careers that have the highest chance of compatibility (Step 2). I'll then run through my approach to psychometric tests, interviews and assessment centres (Step 3). Finally, I'll show you how to audit your work experience and update your skills stack sheet (Step 4).

Chapter 22
How to Use PAFC to Get Ahead

It's easy to read stories about successful people and dismiss them on the belief that you can never achieve what they achieved. After all, they probably didn't undergo the same hardships as you, they probably had it easy—maybe they had supportive and rich parents or they didn't have to battle with any mental health issues.

You try, you fail, and when you hear about someone who succeeded, you dismiss their success as dumb luck and use this belief to live in denial—if you're not as lucky as they are, what hope do you have?

It's an attitude that I've seen in many students and it creates a Catch-22 of sorts. They don't believe that hard work is all that's need, they have convinced themselves that they are powerless to their own misfortune, and so they don't put in the time and the work needed to succeed.

To show you why this is nonsense, let me introduce you to Helena.

At age 24, Helena had a meaningful and engaging career that she was good at. She had secured a job that paid an above average salary and she had full control of her spending habits. Helena had invested £19,000 and was on track to achieve financial freedom well before her retirement age. In June 2019, her life satisfaction rating was 9/10.

After her first year at university, however, it was a different story. She contacted me to ask me for help, as so many other people in her situation have done and continue to do. She was in a time of crisis and was desperate for assistance. She explained that she had a history of mental health issues and as my father had suffered from bipolar disorder, I somewhat understood what she'd gone through.

Despite her problems, Helena had done OK at college and went backpacking around Asia during her gap year. She had also worked in her dad's pharmacy on-and-off over many years.

What started with providing some general advice on study strategy and exam technique, transitioned into me mentoring Helena over 5 years. I saw her transform from an anxious, confused kid into a productive, happy and self-aware person who was comfortable in her own skin.

She is living proof that this process works and that it can work for anyone, even those who feel like their own mind is against them or that they haven't been given the breaks that their fellow students have.

Most of the important decisions Helena took to achieve this success are outlined in the timeline below.

Helena's Timeline

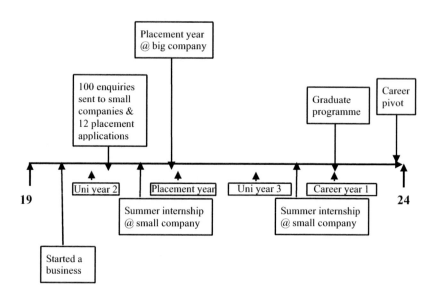

Based on her previous subject choices and exam scores, she had no clear affinity towards words or numbers and her first skills-stack sheet was pretty empty. She didn't know what she wanted to do after graduating, so I reasoned that we needed to employ some shotgun strategies.

However, as Helena was starting her penultimate year of university, we couldn't ignore impeding internship and industrial placement deadlines either. Taking a hybrid approach, we used her skills-stack sheet to generate career ideas and narrowed them down to one. Helena sent over 100 enquiries to small companies in addition to 12 internship/placement applications. She received three offers in response. She also started a business in the summer and made it profitable by month 2. Her second year at university was jam-packed, but it paid off in the end.

Helena deferred her final year at university to do an industrial placement. She converted this into a full-time job that began at the end of the school year. She was good at the work, loved her manager and found some of the work engaging, but it lacked meaning. In her words, the job ticked '1 and a half boxes out of 3' so she continued interviewing to see if there was anything better. Helena did another round of applications until she found a meaningful and engaging career that she was good at.

How to Use PAFC to Get Ahead

I have mentored hundreds of people over the years so I could have used many different stories. I chose to use Helena's story for three reasons:

Firstly, she started remarkably unhappy and finished the happiest, and her career choices had a lot to do with this. If we could turn fulfilment and life satisfaction into currency, Helena had one of the best rags-to-riches stories of them all. I've had other mentees who have achieved greater financial success and are reasonably satisfied with their lives, but none have reached the levels Helena has. Her story shows what happens when you prioritise sustained fulfilment over money.

Secondly, she first came to me as a fairly average person. Helena wasn't one of those wonder kids who achieved straight A's while training to become an Olympic medallist. She had normal working parents, average grades and standard extra circulars. Most people are like her. In fact, I was like her and you are as well. I chose to use her case study because she's relatable.

Finally, Helena found and secured a career that ticked all the boxes within 3 years of graduating. That's fast! It took me 7 years and most of my mentees had to gain experience in various jobs before finding 'the one'.

Over the next four sections of this book, I'm going to use Helena's story along with additional case studies to show you how to efficiently find and secure a fulfilling career that ticks the right boxes. We'll start from the beginning when Helena and I first pieced together a strategy.

Step 1: Pick your Weapon…

Chapter 23
First Steps

Helena: *"I understand all the theory and how I need to find a meaningful, engaging career that I'm good at—but how do I put it all into practice? Where do I start? I've created a skills-stack sheet that I'm happy with."*

Me: *"Good question, and I've had a look at your skills-stack sheet—thanks for sending it. We start with P. We need to pick a strategy for you based on your current situation."*

Helena: *"Shotgun, sniper or hybrid?"*

Me: *"Exactly. To be quite frank, your skills-stack sheet is light but most people your age don't have much experience—I didn't either so don't worry. You need exposure to a broad range of jobs that exercise a broad range of skills within a short space of time. This will add some serious value to your CV."*

Helena: *"Shotgun strategies—starting a business or applying to small companies?"*

Me: *"Yes, but this will be your first opportunity to secure a summer internship or industrial placement. We can't ignore that so a hybrid approach will be best".*

First Steps

Rule of thumb: If you haven't had much work experience, start your own creative venture (ideally a business) and/or work for a small company.

In your first year or non-penultimate second year: Prioritise shotgun strategies, but apply to first year internships if available.

In your penultimate year: Take a hybrid approach. Summer internship and industrial placements are usually only available in your penultimate year and they are far too valuable to miss. Defer your final year to squeeze in an industrial place if you must. Start a creative venture and enquire at smaller companies too. This may seem like a lot, but I see undergraduates like Helena do it every year. There are multiple time-saving hacks you can use when job hunting, which I'll show you in the 'Fire' section.

In your final year: Hopefully you have some experience, understand what your outlier skills are and know what you want to do. If not, extend your 3-year course into a 4-year by applying for a Masters and then applying to internships and industrial placements. You can always cancel the 4th year and bank your bachelor's degree if need be. If this isn't an option, become a sniper and focus on graduate programme applications.

All the advice provided above will work for most people, but there are exceptions. Always consult with qualified careers advisors before making any big decisions.

Chapter 24

Starting a Business & Joining Small Companies

Me: *"Let's start with shotgun strategies. Have you ever started a business or taken any creative risks before?"*

Helena: *"What do you mean by creative risks?"*

Me: *"A creative risk involves coming up with an idea that solves a problem or meets the needs of a group of people, then risking your time and/or money to turn the idea into reality."*

Helena: *"Does starting a blog count?"*

Me: *"Yes!"*

Helena: *"I wrote a few blog posts to boost my UCAS application but I've never really considered starting a business. I thought it's something most people do later in life after gaining some experience."*

Me: *"Not at all. Thanks to technology, it has never been easier to start a business or other creative venture. People your age build successful businesses all the time."*

Am I Too Young to Start a Business?

While accompanying her family on a trip to China, a recent mum with a new-born baby asked a girl called Beau to suggest an English name for her daughter. 'Why does she need an English name and why ask me?' were Beau's initial thoughts. She later learned that many Chinese parents aspire to send their children to European and North American universities. It isn't practical for them to use their Chinese names as 'Westerners' find them difficult to pronounce.

'Fair enough, but why ask me to suggest a name? Can't you just find one yourself?' Beau asked. Finding a suitable English name wasn't easy for the Chinese because of all the censorship and fire walls their government enforce. They can't google 'English names' because they don't have access to Google.

Of all the English names that do filter through, there is often miscommunication. Which is understandable—imagine how difficult it would be to give your kid a suitable Chinese name! As a result, babies are often called inappropriate names like Gandalf and Kelloggs.

Beau saw the opportunity to create a website to help parents find suitable English names. She pitched the idea to her dad and he gave her a small loan to get started. Two years later, she had helped to name 250,000 babies and built a business generating £50,000 in sales a year. She was only 16 years old.

(If you'd like to learn more about Beau, I've put a transcript of my conversation with her at the end of this book)

Helena: *"People like that are just...smart. Plus, she had help from her dad."*

Me: *"You're right, having someone close to you who is an entrepreneur helps, but it isn't a prerequisite. Of those who followed my advice and built successful ventures, like Beau, about half of them had entrepreneurs in their immediate family. The rest achieved success by finding mentors from outside their family. Either way, entrepreneurship has a steep learning curve, so having someone who knows what they're doing will prevent you from making basic mistakes and ensure you follow through."*

Helena: *"It's the following through part which is the problem for me. Like with the blog I started, I didn't get many hits so I just gave up."*

Me: *"Why did you give up?"*

Helena: *"At times I felt that if it was going to work, someone else would have done it already. Sometimes it's the opposite and I think if someone else has already done it so there is no point trying."*

Why you Shouldn't Worry about Competition

The notion that an idea needs to be completely unique for it to work is a fallacy. How many times have you had a eureka moment for a business idea, only for a friend to turn around and say, 'Someone's already done it'? If you're like millions of other ambitious and create individuals, you probably gave up at that point and moved onto the next idea. I've seen people spend a lifetime in this cycle, constantly seeking a unique idea and then giving up when they discover that it's not as unique as they thought.

This is not how the majority of successful entrepreneurs operate. For every business built on a unique idea, there are hundreds, if not *thousands* more built on an idea that has already been done before.

It is much easier to get a product to market if that product already exists in some form. That way, the niche exists, the target-demographic is lying in wait, and you can study your competitors and their successes/failures to understand what works and what doesn't.

Take the tablet PC as an example. The iPad didn't get there first. Microsoft had actually tried to sell the tablet PC to the world many years previous. In fact, while many consumers have completely forgotten about that particular endeavour, the name has stuck, as it was Microsoft who coined the term "tablet PC". They failed because the world wasn't ready for it. But years later, after the success of the iPhone, Apple realised that the market existed and was ready, so they essentially super-sized their iPhone, created a new product, and then pitched it to the same consumers who had bought their previous product.

A close friend of mine built a successful online empire when he was just 17 and became a multi-millionaire in his early twenties. He has created multiple businesses and countless products and none of these were "unique". When I asked him what his process was when starting a new business, he told me, 'I don't try to be the guy who enters an empty room and tries to convince people to join him. I want to be the guy who walks into a crowded room, stands tall, and yells, "Look at me"'.

In other words, his goal is not to create a new product and then focus on building a market for it, but to enter an existing market and do something that gets him noticed. This is the strategy that most entrepreneurs use and it's one you need to keep in mind the next time you reject an idea because it has been done before.

This is a summary of what I told Helena when she suggested that a unique idea was essential for a new business.

Helena: *"I see what you mean—I probably should have kept trying."*

Me: *"Don't worry, most people talk themselves out of starting or give up too soon. However, if you're that one anomaly who* *doesn't give up after the first few hurdles and zig-zags your way to success, you will:*

1. *Exercise a large range of skills within a short space of time.*
2. *Separate yourself from the competition.*
3. *Potentially provide some additional income, or dare I say, grow it into something truly special.*

Why Starting a Business is the Ultimate Shotgun Strategy

Writing my first book required an immense amount of patience and tenacity. My motivation to write ebbed and flowed. I constantly second guessed whether it was worth spending all these hours on something that might fail. What if it didn't sell a single copy? What if it didn't help anyone? I've already told so many people I'm doing this.

"Teenagers don't care about exams—they are only concerned with the opposite sex and music."

"Reading about how to revise won't help anyone—they just need to get on with it."

"You're a bit young—are you really qualified to write a book?"

These were some of many well-intentioned but heart wrenching comments that left me doubting myself for hours. Thankfully, I kept going back to my assumptions and continued writing. I

213

realised why everyone said entrepreneurship was hard. You have to ignore everyone's opinions and trust your own judgement. Conviction is a very personal thing indeed.

Initially, I planned to write the book and park it online. As sales began trickling in and good reviews popped up, my belief in the book's value and its commercial potential sky rocketed. I researched and tried twenty different marketing strategies from leafleting schools to creating online sales funnels. Sales eventually picked up and I thought 'wow this is easy'. I spoke too soon!

As sales continued to grow random problems started appearing everywhere. Amazon deactivated our account and held our money. Someone copied the book and posted it online for free, reducing our sales by 50% overnight. Social media platforms changed their algorithms, making our marketing strategies redundant. Whenever I plugged one hole, another one appeared elsewhere.

To stay afloat I had to continuously innovate and solve problems. There was so much to do and very little time to do it. I had to make decisions off little information and learn quickly. There was no textbook for this stuff!

In just under a year I had been a CEO, marketing director, accountant, finance officer, public relations executive, author, graphic designer and in-house legal dude. I learnt more about myself in this period of time than I had done in 5 years of trading and an entire decade in education. My skills-stack sheet looked completely different!

What did all this show? My i-skills were stronger than my c-skills. Within my i-skills, my numerical skills were stronger than my verbal reasoning. Which was in line with all the psychometric tests that I'd taken over the years. These all confirmed what I more or less already knew. However, I didn't know how strong my creative skills were, particularly when it came to video and photography.

One of the biggest wins I had was developing a set of video campaigns that reached 1.6 million customers over 2 years. These campaigns generated over half a million pounds worth of sales. I wrote the script, recorded the voiceovers and created the animation myself. To achieve a similar level of sales, larger companies often spend tens of thousands of pounds to create marketing content. I did it for £12!

These videos and other content that I developed deeply resonated with our customers. As a result, everyone, including my business partner, praised my creative ability with marketing above all other contributions to the business. When working on marketing, time passed very quickly and it didn't feel like work. Given that I spent my childhood creating videos and photos, this wasn't all that surprising. Part of me always felt that I had a natural aptitude towards creative work, but I needed this experience to prove it.

At university, I picked up the snipe rifle too early and focused on finance. Taking a shotgun approach would have highlighted this area of skill and resulted in better career choices. If my business failed tomorrow and I had to get a job, marketing and creative agencies would be the first places I'd start sending my CV to.

This is why starting an organisation at university and taking it seriously can be a smart move. Not only would it impress employers and separate you from the pack, you will pick up important skills and gain exposure to many different areas of work in a short space of time.

Five out of six people work in the private sector in the UK so you will probably end up in an organisation whose main objective is to make money. That's why I always recommend that undergraduates start a business rather than a non-profit or social enterprise. It's more impressive to employers and you'll learn faster.

Why Starting a Business Helps you Beat your Peers

Everyone respects and admires original thinkers. This is a universal truth that transcends every culture and country. Copying others is easy. However, being someone who acts on nothing but their personal convictions takes bravery and self-confidence. This is why original thinkers are praised everywhere you go.

Having come in contact with various people from all walks of life, I can always identify those who have taken real risk in their lives. They trust themselves more and are comfortable in their own skin. Creative risk-takers speak and carry themselves in a very different way to everyone else. I noticed that same spark when speaking to Beau.

Beau's decision to start a business and stay committed through all the setbacks paid off. Her story went viral and was featured by multiple newspapers across the world. She will always have this story to tell and it will differentiate her from everyone else.

Most importantly, she developed invaluable practical skills that can be applied in the work place and learned what her outlier skills were. Beau's story shows that age isn't a limiting factor when it comes to achieving entrepreneurial, career-boosting success.

Helena: *"Aren't there other ways to differentiate myself or develop skills? Like joining a society?"*

Me: *"Yes—sports, arts and activism are also ways to build an X-factor. Societies too. But society responsibilities end the moment you finish university, you can continue to manage and grow creative ventures for however long you want to. There is also a chance that it turns into something bigger than you ever imagined."*

A Real Chance of a Home Run

"I should start charging you storage fees!"

Anthony joked after Jacob asked to leave his luggage at his flat again. Located between Kings Cross and London Euston, this wasn't the first-time Anthony had been asked to store suitcases and boxes. This is when the lightbulb went off:

"Why don't we create an AirBnB for luggage?"

CityStasher was born! Jacob, in his final year at university and with a graduate job in the bag, worked with his business partner to develop the first version of Stasher. Their idea was to help connect people who wanted to store their items with those who had space in their flats.

Going home for the summer break and need a place to store your stuff? Simply click onto the Stasher website, find an ideal storage location, pay/book and drop your stuff. The person storing your luggage gets a fee and Stasher earns a commission.

Jacob and Anthony started by investing £45 into a service called sharetribe.com to create a basic version of their product. An additional £50 on Google Ads got them their first customer. From the moment they came up with the business idea to their first customer, it took around 3 months of part-time work.

Initially, Jacob and Anthony advertised their own flats to customers. This gave them an opportunity to speak with people who booked using the service and understand what their needs were. They learnt that a lot of them needed storage on a much shorter-term basis than they'd predicted.

Instead of giving up, they pivoted their approach towards becoming a 'left luggage alternative'. People were using them because they were going to concerts, because they were going to stadiums, because they'd just been checked out in the morning and their flight was later and they didn't want to drag their bags around all day.

They were much cheaper than station lockers. After researching those lockers, Jacob realised they could really compete with them. Their next big change came when they decided to work with shops and hotels.

The flat model didn't work so well. For really short-term storage, it was quite annoying to let people in and out twice on the same day unless the owners were in their house doing nothing. Shops were open. They had the space, CCTV and were keen to make more money; same story for hotels. Finally, 7 months after first coming up with the idea, they settled on the business model which led them to success.

Jacob and Anthony raised over £1m in funding from investors, one of which was the CEO and founder of Big Yellow Self

Storage. Stasher is now worth several million pounds. Both Anthony and Jacob are still in their early 20s.

(If you'd like to learn more about Jacob and Anthony's journey, I've put a transcript of my conversation with Jacob at the end of this book)

Helena: *"What about joining a start-up?"*

Me: *"Joining a small company has very similar advantages to starting on your own."*

Work Experience at a Small Company

You still get exposure to a range of tasks and can develop a range of skills quickly. In a start-up, the CEO can be sitting on your left; marketing manager behind; finance on the right and engineer opposite.

Your career capital can grow exponentially if you have the right managers. If they've built a business in the past or come from top companies, work with them.

The job market is very inefficient, and therefore it's possible to use some clever guerrilla tactics to secure good work experience at small companies. Over the past few years, I have used my network to place my most committed mentees in start-ups around London.

"Before 20 years old – be a good student. Before 30 years old – follow somebody – go to a small company. Normally in a big company it is good to learn processing. You are a part of a big machine. But when you go to a small company, you learn the passion, you learn the dreams. You learn how to do a lot of things in a short space of time."
- Jack Ma (Founder of Alibaba)

Starting a Business & Joining a Small Company

Maybe I'm biased because I come from an entrepreneurial family and I'm a business owner. However, I feel most people should start a business at least once in the first quarter of their lives. Given that five out of six people work in the private sector, doesn't starting your own business make sense?

Between the ages of 16 and 25 most people don't have any financial commitments or children to take care of. You can also create your own schedule at university. It's a perfect environment to experiment with ideas and it comes at the perfect time in your life.

If you fail, you lose practically nothing and gain experience that most of the student population don't have. If you succeed and build a multi-million-pound company, like Jacob and Anthony, you achieve financial freedom 40 years earlier than the average person. That's as close to a win-win as you can get.

Achieving any form of commercial success at a young age is

rare. Even if Jacob were to quit the business and apply to a competitive firm, he would stand head and shoulders above his fellow candidates. If Jacob stopped growing the business after achieving a few thousand pounds a month in revenue, this entire experience would have given him an X-factor unique to him and him alone. Think about how much more he would have to talk about in an interview over Joe Bloggs from Oxford:

Interviewer: *"Tell me about your leadership skills."*

Joe: *"I headed up the student union and managed a team of 4 people. Our biggest project was the end of year ball."*

Jacob: *"I started a company called Stasher in 2015, here's what we did…"*

All companies create products and market them; they all deal with legal and accounting etc. The same basic structure is there, so by starting a business you do all of that but on a smaller scale. When I started my publishing business, I had to arrange contracts with suppliers (legal); negotiate rent rates and books; file taxes and do bookkeeping (accounting). Imagine walking into the interview room having done a little of everything in your own business. You will have a much better understanding of how the private sectors works. It's difficult to beat that.

Starting a business is the equivalent to taking a shotgun and shooting right down the middle of the board. In striving to make the business generate sales, developing practical skills and learning about yourself becomes incidental. This is true even if you don't make the business as successful as you wanted it to be. Like Beau, if you generate £50k+ of sales, it will be the cherry on top.

I could write a whole other book on building businesses, but it would go beyond the scope of this one. My hope is to influence those who are on the fence about starting a creative venture to just pull the trigger and figure it out as they go along.

So few undergrads start creative ventures or approach small companies because it's an area that the media doesn't focus on. Searching online for advice on how to start a business at uni or secure a job at a start-up will yield a few short blog posts at best. However, now is one of the best times in history to build career capital in this way.

Across the UK the number of new companies registered last year rose by 5.7% to over 660,000—a record high. Many of these companies are run by competent experienced people who want to grow their businesses. If you show them you're willing to help them achieve their goals, they will hire you and help you develop a broad range of skills.

Helena: *"OK, I'm sold! How do I go about starting a business? When should I get going with this?"*

Me: *"Ideally, right now. Your exams are over and summer holidays are starting soon so this is the best time to get going. Both*

Beau and Jacob started just before their summer holidays. Start brainstorming ideas now—we will get into the details after we discuss sniper strategies and figure out the type of job you should go for."

Chapter 25
Internships, Placements & Graduate Programmes

Not all medium-large companies offer paid work experience. For those that do, they are typically one of the following:

Summer internships: 7-12 weeks

Industrial placement: 10-12 months

Summer internships are available to most undergrads. Industrial placements are usually associated with those on sandwich courses where undergrads work for a year, typically between their 2nd and 3rd year. If you're not on one of these courses, universities are often flexible and can defer your final year. Ask them nicely!

Helena: *"I've strolled around a few careers fairs and am aware that these opportunities exist. My university tutors don't really talk about this stuff much. Also, not many of my friends from the year above secured internships."*

Me: *"This is pretty typical at some universities, and the importance students place on work experience varies each year."*
Helena: *"Why's that?"*

Me: *"Every year group is different and has its own culture. Also, most people make decisions based on what others are doing. Those studying Maths & Economics at my uni went after quality work experience like their life depended on it. While those in my year group studying engineering were pretty laid back about it all. By final year, most of my year group realised that they don't want to be engineers, but completely missed the internship boat and suffered. This is what happens when you kick the can down the road."*

Helena: *"Why don't people realise how important all this is?"*

Me: *"There is no pressure. No one is setting deadlines or looking over your shoulder. No one is saying, 'If you don't figure out what you want to do and get your applications in by 2nd November, you will be kicked out.' No one's communicating the benefits either."*

In a world where there are more graduates than jobs, good brand names will add more value to your CV than some degrees. Also, companies that offer these opportunities are usually large entities that hire competent people, the highest % of our society. Spending several weeks with these people will only add value. Their attitudes, perspectives and skills will rub off on you

This is how you truly turn yourself from a kid to a young adult. Recruiters can smell a graduate who has had valuable work ex-

perience from a mile away. After my internship, I got interviews without going through the whole CV/application she-
bang. One top firm gave me an interview after simply calling
them up!

What most people either ignore or are unaware of, is that the
moment you step into university, the clock starts ticking towards critical deadlines. Internships and placements are a
wormhole into a dimension you want to be in. This wormhole
opens around September and closes in December. Be quick or
you'll miss it!

Why Internships and Placements are a Passport

Many top employers like to try before they buy and fill their
graduate jobs with those who successfully completed internships with them. This is why securing an offer should be a priority.

Some undergrads make it their top priority, even to the detri-
ment of their penultimate year exam marks. They secure an offer, convert the internship into a full-time position and then
make up the ground in their final year. But, ideally, you should
try to balance your degree work with internship and placement
hunting.

Most people only have one shot-one recruitment cycle to get it
right, but there are ways to have two or more shots. After failing
to land a single internship offer in my second year of uni, I

changed my 3-year course to a 4-year. This meant I bought myself another penultimate year to try again. If I didn't receive an internship offer, my plan was to complete an extra year at university and apply to graduate programs. Thankfully, I got it right the second-time round.

Shortly after completing my internship I was offered a full-time position elsewhere. I cancelled my final year, locked in a 3-year bachelor's degree and started my full-time position.

Assuming the area you want to enter offers internships, the closer you get to those deadlines the less time you have to experiment and stack your skills using shotgun strategies. Many graduates end up panicking and firing applications off haphazardly.

Helena: *"So, the plan is to start a creative venture, reach out to small companies, and apply to internships and placements?"*

Me: *"Spot on. A combination of shotgun and sniper strategies."*

Helena: *"Sounds like a lot!"*

Me: *"Don't worry, I'll show you how to manage it all."*

Helena: *"What if I don't secure a full-time offer after all that?"*

Me: *"If you successfully execute all this, your skills-stack sheet will become richer and your CV will become stronger. After 10+ interviews your technique will be miles ahead of other candidates as well. Getting a graduate job shouldn't be problem."*

Graduate Programmes

If you are in your final, don't panic apply or be paralysed in a sea of indecision. You're still only in your early 20s! Try to wrangle yourself another penultimate year like I did and apply for internships. If you can't squeeze another year out, prioritise graduate applications over other shotgun strategies.

If you've graduated already and left university, you have missed the internship boat. However, this shouldn't stop you from applying to graduate programs. Most programs only accept applications from those who have graduated in the past 3 years, so you have a little time on your hands.

Remember that even when you are several years into your career, you still have the option to execute a shotgun strategy in parallel with your normal job. Writing a book and starting a publishing business was definitely not on my agenda while at university, but pulling the trigger was one of the best decisions of my life.

Helena: *"What internships and placements should I apply for?"*

229

Me: *"To answer that question, we need to use your skills-stack sheet and do some career research. After I get a feel for your aptitudes and past, we can then narrow down all the options then select relevant career paths or internships."*

Step 2: Aim

Chapter 26
How to Find 'the one'

Me: *"Before we get into the nuts and bolts, I want to get to know you a little better. I'm going to ask you some deep and personal questions. Is that OK?"*

Helena: *"Sure! Go ahead"*

Me: *"Without meaning to sound cringey, what do you really care about? What do you find meaningful?"*

Helena: *"Not really sure. Well, I care a lot about my family and friends. But beyond that I don't really care for much."*

Me: *"Let's try this from a different angle, can I have a look at your Instagram account?"*

Helena: *"Sure."*

Me: *"Let's scan through the people you follow. Who are your favourite influencers? What type of people do you usually follow?"*

Helena: *"I follow a lot of people who promote positive body image. As you know, I've had a few spells of depression and a* *lot of it had to do with the way I looked. Social media was one of the reasons I felt the way I did, but a few people on Instagram made me feel good about myself. There was one particular model who was very confident in her own skin and I loved her for it. But, why is this relevant?"*

Me: *"When you go through trauma and come out the other side, you automatically join an exclusive club. All the members of this club have been through similar experiences. For the rest of your life, you will be able to relate to each and every one of them because of your common experience.*

Helping any member of your club will always feel more meaningful than helping a random person.

I simply want to find out which clubs you have membership to, as you may be able to pick a career that helps your fellow members."

Helena: *"In that case, I definitely have a lifelong membership to the depression and body image clubs!"*

Me: *"We'll keep that in mind going forward. Let's get back to business: Do you have any careers in mind?"*

Helena: *"Working in insurance would be my best bet. Maybe as an actuary?"*

Me: *"How did you come to that decision?"*

Helena: *"My aunt has been in the industry for 20 years. It pays well and having her on my side will give me a better chance of getting in."*

Me: *"I see your point and there is no harm getting some work experience with her. However, I'm concerned that there might be some 'home bias' in your decision."*

Helena: *"What's that?"*

Me: *"Most students lean towards careers that are familiar to them instead of looking for jobs that are suited to their skills. I knew someone who was unbelievably good at Maths who went for Optometry because his cousin was an optometrist and sold him a dream of owning multiple practices. It didn't work out. Fortunately, he realised where he went wrong and swiftly changed direction towards a career in finance.*

Your family are probably experts in you, but don't assume they are experts in your career. You wouldn't ask Uncle Tony about medicine if he wasn't a doctor, why should careers be any different?"

Helena: *"So, explore other options first?"*

Me: *"Exactly. Insurance might be the right career for you, but we need to start with a blank slate and approach this decision scientifically, which means no bias whatsoever."*

Helena: *"That makes sense and I really do want to make the right decision."*

Me: *"Remember, there is no formula for finding the perfect career. We need to be as objective as possible when looking at your personality traits, aptitudes and history, before comparing them to the demands of various careers. Once we find one that is a good match, you need to pull the trigger and go for it like your life depended on it."*

Helena: *"There seem to be so many options. How do we even begin to narrow them down?"*

Me: *"We narrow them down in two phases."*

Filter Phase: Use advanced career selection software and careers advisors and/or coaches to generate ideas, and narrow these down to 3-5 options.

Select Phase: Conduct detailed online and offline research into those 3-5 options, and choose 1 (max 2) career path(s).

Chapter 27

How to Narrow Down the Options

What's the best way to find a career that fits? Surely there's an app for that? These were the first questions that came to mind when I first started looking for jobs. I'd assumed that someone had figured out, within a reasonable degree of accuracy, how to find the ideal career. It turned out that finding 'the one' career was a lot like finding 'the one' soulmate.

Can Technology Match you with your Ideal Career?

eHarmony is a multi-million-pound company that helps people find love. To access their platform and start matching with people, you first have to answer 436 questions about yourself. They then use this data to find compatible matches. Having collected all this data for the past few decades, they claim to have increased the probability of you finding a long-term partner. I believe them.

If I were to start dating again now, I would most definitely use a service offering an evidence based approach like this. Even a 10% increase in the chances of me finding a suitable date would be worth it.

Some organisations have attempted to construct a similar formula to help people identify suitable careers, but they haven't been around as long as eHarmony. Their claims lack evidence and they are still in the 'data gathering' phase of their lifecycle. However, anecdotal feedback from many students using one particular platform has been strong and I recommend using it.

As of September 2019, Careerexplorer.com by Sokanu is the platform I recommend. The career test, which consists of 310 questions, is designed to measure an extraordinarily large array of factors: your personality, must-haves on the job, can't-stands on the job, a breakdown of hard skills, and much more. Despite its breadth, people complete the assessment in less than 20 minutes on average.

After completing the test one of my colleagues, who is an author and professional copy writer, said the following:

"Careerexplorer.com is brilliant. It told me I should be an author, copywriter or content writer, even when I lied and said I had never worked before and gave no clues about my current job. Careers advisors always told me to get into computers because I had a natural aptitude for them, even though fixing computers drives me around the bend. I might be the exception, but the site was much more accurate for me."

I have followed new academic developments and start-ups closely and do believe that science will help people make better career decisions. If one of these start-ups prove their machine learning algorithms can predict the compatibility of an individual in any given industry, better than the individual themselves or a careers advisor can, I'd change the content in this book. Until then, I recommend that you use a combination of career advisors and software solutions to narrow down your options.

Careers Advisors

What about traditional careers advice? Do those one-on-one counselling sessions with careers advisors help? What about occupational psychology tests?

Last year I went on a BBC London radio show as a study skills expert and was joined by a careers advisor. When asked about the methods used by careers advisors, he spoke about the most popular occupational psychological test used in schools, something he described as the 'Rolls Royce' of occupational psychology.

In this test, candidates are asked to complete questionnaires and various tasks including writing with your non-dominant hand. After 3 hours of testing, you are given compatible career ideas. After reading the research papers written by the psychologists behind this test, I was unconvinced. It seems that many other psychologists are equally sceptical of it too. If this is the Rolls Royce, I'd hate to see what the Skoda is.

Even though the tests are a little wishy washy, traditional face-to-face conversations with qualified careers advisors are still valuable. Not because they are good at suggesting careers, but because most are good at asking questions that get you thinking about your future from different perspectives. Top advisors are also aware of industry trends and can guide you towards professions where you can have a large impact.

You should have two sets of careers advisors/coaches; one set of 'general coaches', who can have discussions like I did with Helena; and one set of 'specialised coaches', who have worked or currently work in the areas you have shortlisted.

To find general coaches, talk to several local career-coaches, including those in your university careers service, and online freelancers on websites like UpWork.com. Within a few conversations, you will instinctively identify which ones know what they are talking about.

Among other activities, careers advisors are trained to assess your core competencies and suggest career paths. Most are aware of their limitations and know you're the only one truly able to determine a suitable path. Good advisors ask the right questions to get you thinking about yourself objectively.

Educational qualifications like 'Masters in Coaching Psychology' and 'Qualifications in Career Guidance (QCG)' are good. However, you should never choose a career coach solely by the letters after their name. Some of the best coaches I encountered didn't have qualifications but had worked in different industries and had a granular understanding of various jobs. They were also very honest when they didn't know about something. Instead of trying to blag, they would say:

"I know someone who works in that industry, I can introduce you."

It's like a GP consulting a textbook or a specialist—it's much more preferable to them simply plucking an answer from thin air and getting a result that is not only useless, but may actually be harmful.

They can't know everything about every career, so don't expect them to be a walking-talking encyclopaedia. It's also a huge positive if your conversation with them triggered ideas, memories and competencies that you previously overlooked, and if they ask questions that no one has asked before.

Ideally, you should look for someone in their 30s or early 40s. You want them to be young enough to relate, but old enough to have experience:

Me: *"Quick fire: Words or numbers?"*

Helena: *"I would say words, but I'm OK at maths too."*

Words, Numbers or Creative?

Most people have an affinity for either words or numbers. What scores did you award yourself in the i-skills section in your sheet? Look at your high school, college and university choices. Do you tend to choose wordy subjects or ones with numbers? Do you prefer essay writing or problem solving?

Shreena achieved Bs and Cs in all her GCSEs apart from English literature and language, where she achieved A*s. Then she did 'wordy' A-levels and went on to study Business and Politics at university, a degree which involved a lot of essay writing. She prefers socialising with friends over watching TV and reads novels on the train. It's safe to say that Shreena should not be an accountant!

She should focus on jobs that require verbal skills over numerical ones. Broadcasting, journalism, human resources, marketing, law, consultancy, merchandising, retail buying and recruitment—these are all sensible options to start with.

She ended up in an investment writing job at a large finance company where she had to create written content for the marketing team. After a trial run in two other positions within the company, Shreena learned more about herself and pivoted towards a traditional marketing job. It took a little wiggling around! Her life satisfaction rating is currently 9/10 and her earnings are in the top 10% of her social circle. It's safe to say her initial choices were correct.

Me: *"Quick fire: Introvert or extrovert?"*

Helena: *"Definitely introvert, all the tests say that too."*

Extro or Intro?

The first letter of your Myers-Briggs profile and the c-skills section of your self-stack sheet can help you narrow down your options further. Even if your i-skills aren't that great, if you've got the gift of the gab, there are a tonne of jobs that you can succeed in.

Aaman was dyslexic with average numerical and verbal reasoning skills; his skills-stack scores were 4 and 5 respectively. However, he had an extroverted personality and an average score of 7 across his c-skills self-stack sheet. Aaman knew that he needed to stay away from jobs that require a lot of numerical problem solving, so jobs in accounting, investment banking and finance went out the window. He needed a job that involved people rather than paper. He told me:

"Everything was pointing towards sales but my dad insisted that I go work for one of the big FTSE 100 firms."

He narrowed down his options to three industries:

1. Management consulting (think McKinsey).
2. Multinational consumer goods companies (think Reckitt Benckiser).
3. Recruitment consulting (think James Caan from Dragons Den).

Deep down he knew that most jobs in the first two groups weren't very suited to his skill set. He was only trying because his dad wanted him to. Unable to pass through the first stages of assessment at top management consulting and multinational consumer products companies, he moved onto his third option: Recruitment consulting.

Nicoll Curtin, an award-winning recruitment agency in London, gave him a shot. Aaman honed his sales skills over the first two years and became one of the top billers in the company. At the age of 23, he was earning over £100,000 a year. He reinvested those earnings into his own property development company that he runs with his dad.

Now Aaman earns twice that amount working 20 hours a week. He goes on 3-4 golf and ski holidays a year. His life satisfaction rating is 8/10. Good career choices? I think so. He was honest about his skill set and carved out a fulfilling life for himself. Approach your career choices in this way and you'll hit a high life satisfaction rating too.

Like Aaman, if talking to people energises you more than solitary problem-solving tasks, finding jobs that are 'people heavy' makes sense. At Nicoll Curtin, Aaman interacted with over 2000 people a year and that suited him well. If you are highly introverted, having to interact and sell to so many people might wane on you over time.

Me: *"There is one part of your skills-stack sheet that really stood out to me. You gave yourself an 8 for negotiation skills and mentioned that you went to trade shows with your dad. Tell me more about this"*

Helena: *"Yes, I went to pharmacy trade shows with my dad and enjoyed analysing all the products. I made an order for a new product to stock in my dad's pharmacy and he let me negotiate. Surprisingly, I managed to get a good discount—Dad was pretty shocked. Not in a 'proud dad' way but genuinely shocked. He's mentioned this scenario multiple times. There are also other random occasions where I had to negotiate and I think it might be something I'm good at.'*

Me: *"I think this is one of your key outlier skills. Do you know what a retail buyer is?"*

Helena: *"No."*

Me: *"I'm sure you've heard of TK Max, Primark, M&S, Tesco, Argos etc. Retail buyers at these companies determine what products to buy and stock—they are negotiators and deal makers."*

Helena: *"That sounds fun, but I don't know if I'd be any good at it"*

Me: *"Don't worry. At this stage, we need to be detectives and trawl through your past looking for clues. Our priority is to* *gather more data about you so that we can make more informed career decisions. Look at how much information you gathered from one experience at a trade show—imagine spending several weeks at a small but fast-growing company."*

Helena: *"Makes sense, so what should I go for then?"*

Me: *"Based on what we discussed, I think we should shortlist retail buying. Have you spoken to any other careers advisors?"*

Helena: *"No"*

Me: *"Go to 2-3 other advisors and take your skills-stack sheet with you. It's important to speak with a diverse group of advisors as they will come up with ideas that I haven't. I can recommend some to you. Be sure to communicate your skills to the advisor in the same structure set out in the skills-stack sheet."*

Helena: *"What's the aim of this?"*

Me: *"To identify patterns and reoccurring themes. If the same career or types of careers keep popping up, then we should explore these further."*

Several weeks later...

Helena: *"I hired a career coach online, she was great! I went to my university careers service and completed the explorelearning.com test too."*

Me: *"Fantastic! What did they come up with?"*

Helena: *"She suggested Patent Law because of my negotiation skills and Chemistry background."*

Me: *"What did the local advisor say?"*

Helena: *"He initially suggested keeping in line with Chemistry—pharmacologist, forensic scientist, toxicologist. etc,. Further into the conversation he suggested law after discussing my negotiation skills."*

Me: *"What about CareerExplore.com?"*

Helena: *"Product manager and journalist were my top matches."*

Me: *"Out of all the options we've discussed, which ones really stand out to you?"*

Helena: *"They have to be product manager and patent law. All the advisors have converged on my negotiation skills but I haven't actually negotiated anything significant, like a hostage situation! I don't know how good a negotiator I am relative to other people and if it's an actual outlier skill."*

Me: *"But you highlighted this in your skills-stack sheet for a* *reason and remembered several examples of when you've negotiated well. You noticed a pattern and the compliments various people made towards this skill.*

You may not be a great negotiator now, but you have the potential to be one. Of course, we might be wrong but we'll only know that after getting you into a real job where you can exercise this skill. Remember we are approaching this as scientists. One hypothesis is that you are a good negotiator, an internship or placement will be our experiment.

Another hypothesis is that a job that helps people with mental health or body image issues will be more meaningful to you. We need an experiment to test this too.

After multiple experiments, you will have a much better idea of what you are good at."

Using Outlier Skills to Choose Career Paths

Like Helena, if you haven't had much work experience, finding outlier skills and narrowing down the options can be difficult. Instinctively, most people know what they are good at, but will struggle to articulate exactly what it is. You may need to pay attention to the faintest pieces of evidence, generalise and generate pretty wild theories. All this will feel rather 'wishy-washy'.

'3 people have complimented me on my negotiation skills, I

*once negotiated well in a tradeshow and outside a nightclub –
therefore I have decent negotiation skills.'*

- Helena

This doesn't seem like good science, but until someone figures
out how to accurately match people with their ideal careers, it's
the best way to get started. It's only the first iteration of many
to come.

How to Narrow Down the Options

Careers advisors will advise based on what you tell them, so be
truthful and show them how you came to your conclusion. It's
OK to say:

*'The last time I was a leader was in scouts 4 years ago when
my team won the summer camp tournament. I think I have decent leadership skills.'*

*'I feel that I'm pretty good with people. I once worked part-time
at a hotel and my manager said I was good with customers'*

-   Before approaching careers advisors, you should be
    able to communicate what your core skills are within a
    short elevator pitch.

-   Use a combination of algorithms and people to nar-
    row down your options down to 3-5 career paths.

- Listen closely to feedback and make notes in your skills-stack sheet.

Helena: *"I've thought about it a lot and have narrowed it down to product manager/retail buying and patent law."*

Me: *"We now need to research these 2 career paths in greater detail and create career-stack sheet for each one."*

Helena: *"What's a career-stack sheet?"*

Me: *"They are 1-2 page documents which provide a summary of each career-path. They should describe the intangible and tangible characteristics of each option."*

Your career-stack sheet should answer 5 key questions:

1. Intangibles:
   a. What skills/personality characteristics separate the strong from the weak in this profession?
   b. What will I do day-to-day?
   c. How meaningful will the work be?
2. Tangibles:
   a. What will my annual salary be for next 15 years?
   b. When will I be financially independent?

Here is an example of a career-stick sheet:

Investment Banking Sales – Morgan Stanley – Career-Stack

Intangibles

What will I do day-to-day?

Convince clients to buy and sell financial products from me at the best price.

Continuously negotiate between traders and clients.

What skills/personality characteristics separate the strong from the weak in this profession?

Fast mental maths – double digit multiplication and basic calculations

Mathematical pitch – instinctively detecting when a number or price is out of line.

Fluid intelligence/quick learning/thinking on feet.

Sales & social skills – superior communication skills, colourful personality, sharp wit.

Thick skin – emotional intelligence/not taking things personally.

Will the work be meaningful?

Indirectly help raise finance for high impact firms, such as alternative energy, technology, biotechnology and robotics.

Tangibles

What will my total estimated earnings be over the next 15 years?

£2.1 million

When will I be financially independent?

2030

Assuming the following:
1. I save and invest 30% of my annual salary
2. Those investments return an average of 6.5% annually

Chapter 28
How to Research Careers Properly

Helena: *"I tried to find answers for the questions in the intangibles section but didn't really get anywhere. For example, when looking for the required skills for patent law, all I got was generic answers like 'team working skills'. Should I just put these in the sheet? Will it be helpful?"*

I used to spend hours researching specific jobs in specific industries, calling and meeting people to ask questions only to receive vague answers. I have lost count of the times someone in human resources gave me a vague response like:

"We're looking for people with good leadership and communication skills."

In my head, I'd be thinking:

"So does everyone else, but that doesn't help me figure out if I'd be a good fit or not!"

Graduate job websites and conversations at careers events can help, but they won't provide the details you need. My main breakthroughs occurred when I spoke face-to-face, one-on-one with people actually working in the areas I was interested in. It's only in private informal settings that the corporate veil is lifted and the truth pours out.

It's crucial that you develop a broad understanding of an industry before meeting those who work within it. Start with Vault Guides and then look at independent organisations that are (ideally) not associated with employers in that industry— Glassdoor.co.uk, Linkedin.com and Quora.com are excellent resources.

Take a look at these two answers on Quora.com in response to the question, 'What type of math is required to become an investment banker?':

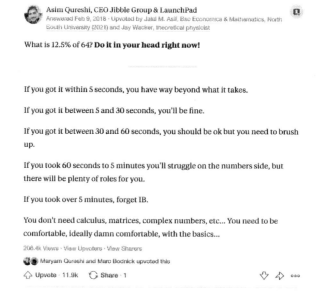

Asim Qureshi, CEO Jibble Group & LaunchPad
Answered Feb 9, 2018 · Upvoted by Jalal M. Asif, Bsc Economics & Mathamatics, North South University (2021) and Jay Wacker, theoretical physicist

What is 12.5% of 64? **Do it in your head right now!**

If you got it within 5 seconds, you have way beyond what it takes.

If you got it between 5 and 30 seconds, you'll be fine.

If you got it between 30 and 60 seconds, you should be ok but you need to brush up.

If you took 60 seconds to 5 minutes you'll struggle on the numbers side, but there will be plenty of roles for you.

If you took over 5 minutes, forget IB.

You don't need calculus, matrices, complex numbers, etc... You need to be comfortable, ideally damn comfortable, with the basics...

206.4k Views · View Upvoters · View Sharers

Maryam Qureshi and Marc Bodnick upvoted this

Upvote · 11.9k   Share · 1

How to Land Your Dream Graduate Job

 Pedro Miranda, Former investment banker @GoldmanSachs
@CreditSuisse

Updated Mar 20, 2018 · Upvoted by Andrew Carr, MS Computer Science & Mathematics,
Brigham Young University (2020) and Yair Livne, Master's Mathematics, Hebrew
University of Jerusalem (2007)

You don't need any esoteric math knowledge as Asim Qureshi points out. But
you need perfect number pitch (trademark).

What the hell is that?

It is the mathematical equivalent of Absolute pitch - Wikipedia ⊕ in music.

That means that numbers out of place bother you to the point that drive you
crazy. Just like when you listen to a kid playing the piano and when s/he hits the
wrong note it hurts your ears.

Let me explain how it happens. It is 11pm and you are sipping espresso #11 for
that day. You see on a presentation that McDonalds had $12 billion in earnings
last year. That would go by the untrained person because MCD is a very large
company and $12 billion is a very large number.

But it immediately catches your attention. That number jumps out of the page.
Because you *know* that large fast food companies trade at about 25 earnings and
that would mean that McDonalds has a $300 billion market cap. But you *know*
ExxonMobil is a $300 billion company and there is no way that MCD is larger
that XOM. That $12 billion is wrong.

All this happens in your head in less than 30 seconds. You look up the correct
number (it is about $5 billion), fix the presentation and continue.

Perfect number pitch allows you to quickly spot mistakes even if you had no
sleep in the last 30 hours.

Information like this is gold. Enter these under the 'Skills required' column in your career stack sheet. After developing a
basic understanding of each career, you should look to interview people who work within the industry.

Where to Find Industry Professionals and Career Coaches

Your personal network of friends and family should always be your first port of call. Those who know you personally are almost always more likely to lend more of their time and provide honest advice.

Both offline and online networking are second on the list. Career fairs, talks hosted by companies, seminars hosted by university societies and private companies are all good places to meet people. Talks and seminars are usually followed by networking sessions where you can ask industry professionals questions.

When company staff talk at a career event they give a watered-down version of the truth and it's easy to understand why. Put yourself in their shoes—imagine that you were asked to talk about your job to 100 undergraduates, with your team and managers present. Would you tell the whole truth or make your job sound rosy? As a naïve kid, I used to take everything they said at face value. Make sure you don't.

As for online networking, hiring industry experts and career-consultants on websites like clarity.fm is another good option. Most people advertise to offer services to business and don't expect to receive enquiries from teenagers asking for career advice. It is a largely untapped way of networking and many of my mentees have had good results from this approach.

What to Ask Industry Professionals

An industry professional's time is precious—you don't want to waste it asking them basic questions you could have found online. Helena shouldn't be asking:

1. What exactly is patent law?
2. What does a patent lawyer do?
3. How big is your company?

Instead, she should be focusing on them and their personal experience. She should have asked broad questions like this:

1. If you could go back in time, what advice would you have given yourself?
2. What separates a good patent lawyer from a bad one?
3. Is there a personality trait or quality that all good patent lawyers share? If so, what is it?

as well as specific questions like:

1. What do you do on a day-to-day basis?
2. What were you working on yesterday/today?
3. When you first became qualified, what did a typical day look like?

Whenever I spoke to people over the phone or met them face-to-face, I'd first let them know why I was calling and then I'd take control of the conversation by saying:

"I don't want to take up too much of your time so I've got a set of questions here that I'd like to ask you first, if that's OK?"

They appreciated the structure and efficiency. It's also much easier and less demanding to sit and answer a few questions than it is to carry the conversation, and as they're doing you a favour, you need to make things easy for them.

How to Research Careers Properly

If you are in a similar position to Helena and don't have much work experience, this whole process will take some time. You may need to continuously go back to your general careers advisor as there are so many different jobs and industries to choose from. At times, it will feel like you're making your way through a complicated maze continuously hitting dead ends.

Develop a base level of understanding of the industry in which the job exists. Then, learn about the job itself by using Vault Guides independently owned platforms or resources unaffiliated with the industry.

Use both offline and online networking to develop a granular understanding of the job. There is no substitute for a one-on-one face-to-face conversation with a seasoned professional. Getting in front of them, building rapport and asking the right questions will help you in the best way possible.

Chapter 29
Tallying up your Tangibles

Helena: *"Where's the best place to look for salary progression?"*

Me: *"You're lucky, salary information used to be really difficult to get a hold of. Now Glassdoor.co.uk and a Google search can show you most of what you need. I'd always check these figures with real people whenever you can."*

You have to be very tactful when it comes to talking about money. Employers feel that staff highly motivated by money won't be good at their job and won't be loyal to the company as they'll always be looking for higher paying jobs. As an employer myself, I know that everyone is working for money but employees that are intrinsically good at certain tasks and have a genuine interest in our customers will perform better and make my life easier.

"I have a unique family situation so I do need to consider long-term career progression and compensation alongside everything else. I know what my compensation will be in year 1, but what am I looking at from year 2 onwards?"

This is what I asked multiple recruiters before applying to internship and graduate jobs. My primary goal was to get a feel for how much I was going to earn over a 10-15 year period. Using this value, I calculated approximately how much I could invest over that period of time and when I'd become financially independent.

Of course, the earnings information I found was only an estimate as it would be dependent on my performance at work and a number other factors. However, with most professions, you can estimate how much you'll earn over several years within a reasonable degree of accuracy. This is especially true for jobs that do not pay commission or bonuses. For example, if you become a merchandiser for a large beauty company, almost 100% of your compensation will be your base salary.

As a recruitment consultant or an estate agent, your base salary will be lower but you will have the opportunity to earn large commissions. Income from two employees who are the same age or career level can be very different. When evaluating these career paths and other commission based jobs, be conservative with your estimate as it's difficult to determine how you'll perform until you start working.

How do I Estimate my Future Earnings?

The first step is to pick a timeframe. I chose 3, 5, 10, 15 years. Then you need to calculate how much money you will earn from each career path over these periods of time. This is going to take research and digging around. In an ideal world, you should be able to call up the HR department of a company you are interested in and have the following conversation:

You - *"I'm thinking of applying for your graduate position for xyz. I think I'll enjoy the job and will be good at it. I'd just like to get an idea of career progression and the compensation I'd receive over 3, 5, 10 and 15 years. Can you help me?"*

HR - *"That will be difficult because everyone's career paths are different. It will depend on your performance."*

You - *"I understand, but I really do think some indication of compensation would help me decide. How about the average income earned by graduates for this department in their first 3 years?"*

HR - *"That's doable. You're looking at £29k, £31k and £35k. It will be difficult to give you figures beyond that."*

You - *"Brilliant, that's really helpful! For years 4 and beyond, do you have high-median-low range of compensation for employees"?*

HR - *"You are really putting me on the spot here but, fine:*
Year 4: £37k - £43k - £48k
Year 5: £39k - £49k - £55k
Year 6: £42k - £54k - £64k
Year 7: £42k - £56k - £68k

Year 15: £48k - £89k - £123k

You - *"That's really helpful. Finally, do you have any case studies of graduates and their career progression across 15 years?"*

HR - *"I'm glad I could help and yes. I'll send those over to you by e-mail right away."*

If only it were that simple. There are a tiny proportion of forward-thinking companies like Netflix who are completely open about how much they pay employees. Some human resources departments at companies can give you a rough idea, but the vast majority won't reveal this information and you'll have to piece it together yourself by:

1.   Using online resources like Glassdoor.co.uk.

2. Contacting past or current employees through LinkedIn and networking events.

3. Speaking to recruitment agents.

Creating your Financial Forecasts

Remember Salah from chapter 13? Between the ages of 21 and 40, he saved between 36% to 49% of his salary. He started a sales job straight out of university and earned £26,000 in his first year (base salary + bonus) and by the age of 36 he was earning six-figures.

Salah earned a total of £1.43m over 20 years and placed 44% of this amount into an investment account. His investments generated an average annual return of approximately 7%. As a result, by the age of 40, Salah had a total net worth of £1.06m in his savings account and achieved financial independence 20 years before his official retirement age.

The reason I ask mentees to estimate future earnings is to reinforce the importance of saving and determine when they will have the option to retire or semi-retire. By compiling a simple spreadsheet, you will see the effect your annual savings will have on your future. Spending less, earning more and staying disciplined with your investments over a long period of time will reward you. Take a look at Helena's earnings forecast:

Helena – Patent Lawyer – Forecast

Age	Salary (In)		Expenses/Tax (Out)		Savings		Investment Account Balance	
44	£	182,869	£	128,008	£	54,861	£	1,296,510
43	£	177,542	£	124,280	£	53,263	£	1,165,868
42	£	172,371	£	120,660	£	51,711	£	1,044,700
41	£	167,351	£	117,146	£	50,205	£	932,384
40	£	162,477	£	113,734	£	48,743	£	828,337
39	£	157,744	£	110,421	£	47,323	£	732,013
38	£	153,150	£	107,205	£	45,945	£	642,901
37	£	148,689	£	104,082	£	44,607	£	560,522
36	£	144,358	£	101,051	£	43,307	£	484,428
35	£	140,154	£	98,108	£	42,046	£	414,197
34	£	93,436	£	65,405	£	28,031	£	349,438
33	£	90,714	£	63,500	£	27,214	£	301,791
32	£	88,072	£	61,651	£	26,422	£	257,818
31	£	85,507	£	59,855	£	25,652	£	217,274
30	£	83,016	£	58,112	£	24,905	£	179,926
29	£	55,344	£	38,741	£	16,603	£	145,560
28	£	53,732	£	37,613	£	16,120	£	121,086
27	£	52,167	£	36,517	£	15,650	£	98,560
26	£	50,648	£	35,454	£	15,194	£	77,850
25	£	49,173	£	34,421	£	14,752	£	58,831
24	£	32,782	£	22,947	£	9,835	£	41,389
23	£	31,827	£	22,279	£	9,548	£	29,629
22	£	30,900	£	21,630	£	9,270	£	18,855
21	£	30,000	£	21,000	£	9,000	£	9,000

This model assumes that Helena:

1. Receives a training contract at a law firm straight after university.

2. Saves 30% of her total annual salary over the next 20+ years.

3. Achieves a 50% pay rise after qualifying as a patent lawyer at the age of 25.

4. Sees her salary increase at an average of 7-8% annually.

5. Invests all her savings into global stock and bond markets.

6. Sees the value of her savings go up by an average of 6.5% per year.

As you can see, this model is fairly simple and there are a number of factors which are difficult to predict. Helena does eventually want to get married and have children. She didn't include the income of a future partner/spouse or the additional expenses/lost earnings of having kids. She has conservatively assumed these factors balance out but, in reality, Helena and her spouse will probably save much more than what's shown on the spreadsheet.

Tallying up your Tangibles

Helena initially gathered her earnings information from online platforms and careers websites. Then, a qualified patent lawyer verified her assumptions. In the research process, she realised that moving to a new law firm a few years after qualifying could result in a 10-20% pay rise.

Based on these assumptions, Helena estimated that she would achieve financial independence at the age of 44 as a patent lawyer.

With close to £1.3m invested, she could withdraw approximately £50,000 a year for the rest of her life and still see the total value of her savings grow.

Over these 20+ years, a percentage of her total income will be put into another pot that Helena cannot touch until she reaches a certain age. This is called her 'pension'. As it stands she will only be able to access that money by the age of 55, however this will change to 57 by 2028 and quite possibly 60+ by 2040. This means she could potentially semi-retire or fully retire 16-20 years earlier than the average.

At this age, she may have a long-term partner with whom she can go travelling for a few years without any financial concerns. She might have children who are approaching an age where they need her time and support. Her choices now will give her the freedom to do all that.

Helena also ran the numbers for a career in retail-buying:

Helena – Retail Buyer – Forecast

Age	Salary (In)	Expenses/Tax (Out)	Savings	Investment Account Balance
54	£ 90,930	£ 68,197	£ 22,732	£ 1,300,169
53	£ 89,147	£ 66,860	£ 22,287	£ 1,199,471
52	£ 87,399	£ 65,549	£ 21,850	£ 1,105,337
51	£ 85,685	£ 64,264	£ 21,421	£ 1,017,359
50	£ 84,005	£ 63,004	£ 21,001	£ 935,153
49	£ 82,358	£ 61,768	£ 20,589	£ 858,358
48	£ 80,743	£ 60,557	£ 20,186	£ 786,638
47	£ 79,160	£ 59,370	£ 19,790	£ 719,673
46	£ 77,608	£ 58,206	£ 19,402	£ 657,167
45	£ 76,086	£ 57,065	£ 19,022	£ 598,841
44	£ 74,594	£ 55,946	£ 18,649	£ 544,431
43	£ 73,132	£ 54,849	£ 18,283	£ 493,692
42	£ 69,649	£ 52,237	£ 17,412	£ 446,394
41	£ 66,332	£ 49,749	£ 16,583	£ 402,800
40	£ 63,174	£ 47,380	£ 15,793	£ 362,645
39	£ 60,165	£ 45,124	£ 15,041	£ 325,682
38	£ 57,300	£ 42,975	£ 14,325	£ 291,681
37	£ 54,572	£ 40,929	£ 13,643	£ 260,428
36	£ 51,973	£ 38,980	£ 12,993	£ 231,723
35	£ 49,498	£ 37,124	£ 12,375	£ 205,380
34	£ 47,141	£ 35,356	£ 11,785	£ 181,226
33	£ 44,896	£ 33,672	£ 11,224	£ 159,099
32	£ 42,758	£ 32,069	£ 10,690	£ 138,850
31	£ 40,722	£ 30,542	£ 10,181	£ 120,338
30	£ 38,783	£ 29,087	£ 9,696	£ 103,435
29	£ 36,936	£ 27,702	£ 9,234	£ 88,018
28	£ 35,178	£ 26,383	£ 8,794	£ 73,975
27	£ 33,502	£ 25,127	£ 8,376	£ 61,203
26	£ 31,907	£ 23,930	£ 7,977	£ 49,603
25	£ 30,388	£ 22,791	£ 7,597	£ 39,085
24	£ 28,941	£ 21,705	£ 7,235	£ 29,567
23	£ 27,563	£ 20,672	£ 6,891	£ 20,969
22	£ 26,250	£ 19,688	£ 6,563	£ 13,219
21	£ 25,000	£ 18,750	£ 6,250	£ 6,250

This model assumes Helena:

1. Saves 25% of her total annual salary over the next 30+ years.

2. Sees her salary increase at an average of 4% annually.

3. Invests all her savings into global stock and bond markets.

4. Sees the value of her savings go up by 6.5% per year on average.

Based on these assumptions, Helena estimated that she would achieve financial independence at the age of 54 as a retail buyer.

Contrary to the legal profession, income growth in the retail sector is gradual and salaries generally don't exceed £70k. In 30 years that ceiling will most likely increase to £90k due to inflation. Helena could potentially semi-retire or fully retire 6-8 years before being able to access her personal pension pot and 16-20 years before being able to access her government pension pot.

Tallying up your Tangibles

Helena might spend everything she earns in the first year, realise that she likes the finer things in life and then decide that she has no interest in saving for the future. YOLO, right? She might love her job and never see herself retiring until she's in her 60s, regardless of how much her investments are worth. An inheritance might come early and completely alter her life plan. She might get divorced and have to split the investment account with a partner. She may even win the lottery.

Any number of scenarios could play out. So why try to forecast a future that can change so drastically?

Planning gives you a road map, something tangible you can hold on to. No matter how much your path deviates, you know that plan is based on sound logic and you will naturally revert to it in times of indecision.

Also, it's important to see how both earning progression and spending can affect your retirement plans. Financial freedom is worth it for the majority of people.

Many undergraduates choose their careers solely based on earning potential. This is a mistake. However, ignoring money completely is also a mistake. Salary should never be looked at on its own or as a scorecard of some sort. Rather, it should be looked at alongside spending and in the context of achieving financial independence. This is why you should take some time to create these spreadsheets, play around with the numbers and record the results in your career-stack sheets.

Chapter 30
Aim

Helena: *"I researched both options in detail and spoke to at least one industry professional in each area. I did my best to be objective, as you said."*

Me: *"Let's take a look at your career-stack sheets and decide how to proceed."*

Aim

Patent Law – Barker Brettell – Career-Stack

Intangibles

What will I do day-to-day?

Mostly independent reading/research and writing.

Can an invention be patented? - estimating the chances of success and making judgement calls.

Advising clients and communicating with colleagues.

Understanding and discussing technical information (chemical formulae).

Potential and occasional public speaking – presentations and courtroom trials.

What skills/personality characteristics separate the strong from the weak in this profession?

Verbal reasoning – ability to read large volumes of written prose filled with jargon and to extract the most important/relevant pieces of information.

Oral articulation – explaining complex concepts clearly.

Adapting explanations to people with different levels of under-standing.

How meaningful will my work be?

Using medicine as an example: protect inventions in the phar-maceutical industry, enabling manufacturers to mass produce life enhancing/extending drugs

Tangibles

What will my total earnings be for next 15 years?

£976,473

When will I be financially independent?

44

Assuming the following:
1. I save & invest 30% of my annual salary.
2. Those investments return an average of 6.5% annu-ally.

Aim

Retail Buyer – TK Max – Career-Stack

Intangibles

What will I do day-to-day?

Analyse (calculate and compare) sales data – be able to answer questions like, Why did this store sell more than that one?

Negotiate with suppliers on quantity and pricing.

Choose designs for in-store promotional displays, online and offline catalogues, potentially direct models, photographers and graphic designers on aesthetics.

Check and approve samples from suppliers.

Order stock using financial tools like LOCs (letter of credit).

What skills/personality characteristics separate the strong from the weak in this profession?

Basic maths – calculating gross margin, mark-up, etc.

Negotiation and relationship building.

Assertiveness and forthright personality.

How meaningful will my work be?

Could potentially manage products that help people with body image problems.

Tangibles

What will my annual salary be for next 15 years?

£539,464

When will I be financially independent?

Age 54

Assuming the following:
1. I save & invest 25% of my annual salary.
2. Those investments return an average of 6.5% annually.

Helena: *"I went back and forth over all the different options suggested by you and other careers advisors. I also looked at others like copywriting and journalism. It's really interesting to see how much I can earn over a 15-20 year period."*

Me: *"What did you find out?"*

Helena: *"Surprise surprise, law pays the most!"*

Me: *"Anything else?"*

Helena: *"Over a 15-year period, I would earn nearly twice as much in some areas of law than I would in merchandising and nearly three times as much as a career in journalism. That's one of the reasons I put journalism to the bottom of my list. I get what you're saying about aiming towards financial independence and I don't know if I'll have the spending discipline to get there, but going for a career that will make me less than £500k over the next 15 years won't give me the option. I don't think I'd be able to save much at all. Retail isn't as lucrative as law but I can still get near enough to the £1m mark by my late 40s."*

Me: *"Great work!"*

Helena: *"Looking at salaries and career progression does clear things up on the money front. It's good to know these things in advance rather than being surprised later."*

Intangibles

Me: *"If your total earnings over 15 years were the same for both career paths, which one would you pick?"*

Helena: *"I'd say retail buying/merchandising because of those experiences that I had with my dad. But, it's really difficult to tell!"*

Me: *"That's OK. Talking through the pros and cons of each path is more productive than you think."*

Helena: *"I'm a little concerned about the maths involved with retail buying."*

Me: *"You do need to be reasonably good at numbers, however we aren't talking about complex maths. Understanding key retail terminology is half the battle. You can use those figures to analyse sales data. If your numerical reasoning scores were less than 4, I'd be a little more worried but you'll be fine. Calculators exist for a reason!"*

Helena: *"Which one do you think I should go for?"*

Me: *"I think buying/merchandising is your best bet for this year."*

Helena: *"Really, why?"*

Me: *"Law in itself is a very competitive field. IP and patent law is even more specialised and competitive—you won't find many companies that offer internships and there aren't many firms that offer graduate traineeships. Of those that do, only a few of them look for Chemistry backgrounds and many value masters/PHDs. 60% of patent attorneys have these qualifications.*

In other words, securing a training contract in that industry will require a full-on sniper approach. You'll have to invest a lot of your time into getting your CV to a point where it's 'ready'. Given that you haven't had much work experience, along with the competitive nature of law, means it's too much of a gamble. What if you invest the next 3 years of your life to become an IP solicitor only to realise that you don't enjoy it? You would never have tried any other profession and will be constantly wondering if the grass is greener on the other side. If you had come to me after a gap year placement in retail and a few other work placements, I would have said, 'Right, let's get the sniper out and aim for IP law'. We don't have enough data YET to make that gamble.

It's for these reasons that, in my opinion, you should aim at buying/merchandising roles and jobs related to them. What are your thoughts?"

Helena: *"I see what you are saying."*

Me: *"By this time next year, if you have completed an internship at a large retailer and some additional work experience, that would be a big win."*

Helena: *"That does sound pretty good."*

Me: *"I suggest we send out 10-15 internship applications followed by about 100+ enquiries to smaller consumer product companies. If we get some early traction with those and have time, then send some speculative applications to law firms."*

Helena: *"That sounds like a lot of work!"*

Me: *"Securing an internship will take the most time but sending enquiries to smaller companies is fairly systematic. There are lots of hacks that can save you time and I'll show you what to do."*

Aim

High Barrier-to-Entry Jobs

Part of me wanted to tell Helena, *"If you want to be an IP lawyer, you should go for it—lets apply to corporate law internships, send enquiries to 100+ legal practices and look at potential PHDs/masters—you can do anything you put your mind to."*

If life was a cute coming-of-age film and we all acted like everything was in reach and the world was your oyster, that would be true and she would be a successful lawyer within a year or two. But it's not, and that would have been very bad advice.

One decent internship or work experience can produce multiple career revelations. Helena may find an area of work that she loves but had never even considered before. She simply won't know until she dips her feet in.

High barrier-to-entry jobs tend to have their own eco-systems. Once you're in that system, it's difficult to look out and experiment with other careers or areas. Try talking to a medic about technology and finance. It will go way over most of their heads because their industry demands so much attention and the high barriers they had to climb over to get in are now preventing them from looking outwards.

280

Me: *"Hopefully, if your internship at the retailer goes well, you will have one graduate offer in the bag. If it doesn't work out, having that internship on your CV will make it easier to get a grad job at another retailer. If you still feel the grass will be greener in law, you can switch your strategy and go all-in."*

Helena: *"Wouldn't it look a bit funny on my CV if I have retail buyer in there then all of a sudden I want to be a lawyer?"*

Me: *"Not if you explain it. I had lined up an accounting internship in China at one point and was asked about it in a first-round interview. They suggested that I seemed a little 'unfocused' and asked me why I was applying to Asset Management. I told them, 'Everyone who has ever given me career advice has said that I should try everything and get a variation of experience whilst I'm young.'*

Both interviewers nodded in agreement and moved on to the next question. I was later invited back to the final round of interviews"

Helena: *"Wow, OK"*

Me: *"Most people panic and try to blag unexpected questions like that but you'll be surprised how much value simply telling the truth brings."*

Focus on One or Spread your Bets?

As a rule of thumb, if you are in your first or penultimate year, spreading your bets between 2 areas of interest is OK. Do this only if you are torn between two types of jobs or if your 'home-run' option is ultra-competitive.

IP law is highly competitive and there was a very real possibility that Helena wouldn't have gotten a training contract. If she swings and misses, at least she has a back-up career that she has a strong chance of enjoying. There is nothing wrong with hedging your bets in this way.

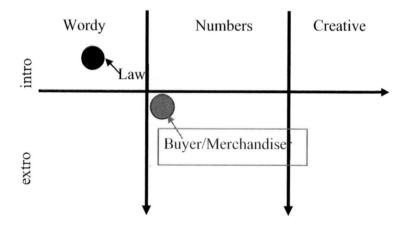

Helena identified with being an introvert who was equally good with numbers and words. By completing sophisticated tests and utilising the services of a careers advisor, she narrowed down her options to two.

As she was in her penultimate year with limited work experience, she decided to aim at a lower-barrier to entry options first to learn more about herself and add value to her CV. Her goal was to secure both a structured internship/placement at large company and work experience at a smaller high-growth firm.

Aim

The first stage of this decision-making process is rather qualitative and unscientific. By gathering all the data about yourself in your self-stack sheet, you have completed 25% of the work. The remaining 75% comes from researching potential career paths, including those that you have zero interest in. This can take several weeks of work. With my mentees, I set them tangible research targets like 'read 200 job prospectuses in 2 weeks' and then I check their Google search history. I expect to see searches like:

"What does a strategy consultant do?"

"What is investment banking?"

"What does Diageo do?"

"Example day of a GP."

Set yourself similar targets and read through job prospectuses online. Always keep a printed version of your self-stack sheet in front of you when job searching. Look for common phrases or themes between your sheet and any information provided by employers.

After reading 200+ prospectuses, 5+ Vault Guides and a few trips to your career service you should have between 3-5 jobs that match your self-stack sheet. Armed with these options, you can now build a career-stick sheet for each one.

This is where most undergraduates go into paralysis. Narrowing down your options to a set of industries or jobs that suit your skills is a reasonably objective approach. However, you still have a lot of options in front of you. Reading Vault Guides, going to networking events and then 'picking the one that feels OK' is a little wishy-washy, but it works.

You aren't picking the job that you're doing for the rest of your life. This is your first shot of many and all you're doing is making an educated guess as to where to aim. If you send a bunch of applications, land a 3-week placement at a small broadcasting company and then do a horrible job, it isn't the end of the world. You just need to use the experience to update your skills-stack sheet and refine your aim on the next go.

1. Use your skills-stack sheet to narrow down your options.

2. Research those roles in more detail and narrow it down further into 2-5 options.
3. Create career stack-sheets for those options.
4. Use skills-stack and career-stack sheets to pick 1 or 2 areas of work.

Step 3: Fire

Chapter 31

How to Get an Offer in the Bag

Once you've picked a job or industry, you'll need to jump head-first into that ecosystem and start learning everything you can about how it works. If you've picked two or more different areas, you will need to jump into multiple ecosystems.

Begin by looking for a mentor who is currently working in the industry and is willing to lend their time. If you find the right person, you will learn much faster than your competition. An experienced insider is much more valuable than a Google search result.

Helena read Vault Guides, scoured the internet, went to company talks and found two mentors in the industry. To secure herself an internship and work experience, she needed to:

1. Identify potential target organisations.

2. Create truthful answers to core competency questions.

3. Maintain or build an X-factor.

4. Create an attention-grabbing CV.

5. Find and apply to 10+ internship/placement pro-
    grammes at large companies.

6. Find and send enquiries to 100+ smaller companies.

7. Convert as many interviews as possible into job of-
    fers.

This is what execution looks like. Some parts will be gruelling
while others can be systemised into any easy quick process.
There will be parts of this journey you will enjoy too, particularly that moment your hard work pays off and you receive an
offer!

Chapter 32
Identify Target Organisa-tions & Build a Database

Helena: *"I liked the look of some companies that I came across during my initial research. Should I go ahead and apply to them?"*

Me: *"Not just yet. You're going to come across hundreds of companies in the retail and merchandising industry over the next few months. We first need to create a database on Excel to keep you organised."*

Most grads tend to jump headfirst into applications without much planning. Creating an Excel sheet that lists all your target organisations and their requirements will help you prioritise. The Excel sheet should have:

1. A summary sheet which shows a snapshot of your progress with all the applications (you can download this at AcademicUnderdogs.com/tools):

Big Companies

	Organisation name	Position	Link	Application Open Date	Application Deadline	Application Requirements	Application progress	Date applied	Status
1	TK Maxx	Placement		1st Aug 2019	20th Feb 2020	App questions, CV & cover letter	50%	N/A	Pre-application
2	M&S	Placement		Open	Ongoing	App questions & CV	25%		Pre-application
3	Tesco	Placement		Open	Ongoing	App questions & CV	25%		Pre-application
4	YSL	Placement		Open	Ongoing	App questions, CV & cover letter	50%		Pre-application
5	Sainsbury's	Placement		Open	Ongoing	App questions & CV	0%		Pre-application
6	Lidl	Placement		Open	Ongoing	App questions & CV	0%		Pre-application
7	Debenhams	Placement		Open	Ongoing	App questions & CV	50%		Pre-application
8	Aldi	Placement		Open	Ongoing	App questions, CV & cover letter	25%		Pre-application
9	GSK	Placement		Ongoing	Ongoing	App questions, CV & cover letter	50%		Pre-application
10	Eaton	Placement		1st Aug 2019	Ongoing	App questions, CV & cover letter	25%		Pre-application

Small Companies

Lead strength		Organisation name	Contact	Link	Application Requirements	Engagement 1	Engagement 2	Engagement 3	Engagement 4	Engagement 5	Engagement 6	Engagement 7
	1	Kelly Group	N/A	N/A	No formal application	e-mail	e-mail	call				
	2	Kiki Wiki	Selena Khan	N/A	No formal application	e-mail	e-mail	call				
	3	Elysium Ltd	Harry Jiles	N/A	No formal application	e-mail	e-mail (responded)	call				
	4	Bella	Jake Lawson	N/A	No formal application	e-mail	email					
	5	Selly Kellins LLC	Nik	N/A	No formal application	e-mail	call					
	6	Cammy	Priya Shah	N/A	No formal application	e-mail	e-mail	email				
	7	Santella	N/A	N/A	No formal application	e-mail	call	call				
	8	No Sweat	DJ	N/A	No formal application	e-mail						
	9	Batino	Emma Davis	N/A	No formal application	e-mail	e-mail	e-mail				
	10	Troove	Adam Smith	N/A	No formal application	e-mail						
	11	Tinampa	Kunal Tanna	N/A	No formal application	e-mail	call					
	12	Soisk	Mohammed	N/A	No formal application	e-mail						
	13	Trilogy	Timothy Burns	N/A	No formal application	e-mail						
			Oliver Yu	N/A	No formal application	e-mail						

Sheet tabs: Summary | TK Maxx | M&S | Tesco | YSL | Sainsbury's | Lidl | Debenhams | Aldi | GSK | Eaton | Kelly Group | +

and

2. Additional sheets dedicated to each organisation:

Summary	TK Maxx	M&S	Tesco

The summary sheet should have the following columns:

Big Company Columns:

Organisation Name, Link, Position, Application Open Date, Application Deadline, Application Requirements, Application Progress, Date Applied & Status, Link.

Small Company Columns:

Organisation Name, Link, Contact, Application Requirements, Engagement 1, Engagement 2, Engagement 3, Engagement 4, Engagement 5, Engagement 6, Engagement.

Create one additional sheet for every organisation you add and hyperlink the company name to that sheet:

Identify Target Organisations & Build a Database

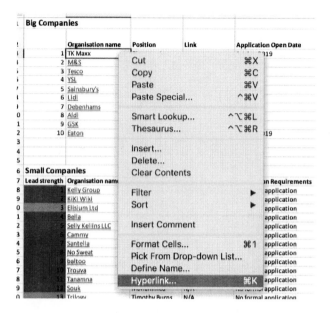

Hyperlink the organisation name to its respective sheet.

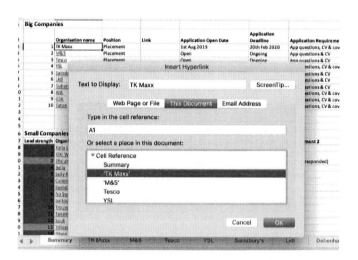

Helena: *"I've created my sheet. Where should I start?"*

Me: *"Start with internships and placements"*

How to Find Relevant Grad Jobs, Internships and Placements

The first step in this process is to research all the big companies offering internships and graduate positions in your chosen field of interest. Use the internet and work through the top 10 results on Google. Once you've done that then you can switch to resources like milkround.com, targetjobs.co.uk and The Times Top 100 Graduate Employers.

If you find yourself drifting down online wormholes and studying jobs that have nothing to do with your choices or skill-set, don't worry, it's normal. It can actually be beneficial—you may stumble upon something interesting. Just remember to focus most of your attention on the career path you have picked from your initial research.

When you identify an employer who offers the job you want, register and login to their application portals and then enter all the necessary information into your tracking sheet. Copy and paste the key questions they ask into the additional tabs on your Excel sheet.

	TK Maxx			
1	**TK Maxx**			
2				
3		Question	Max Words	Answer
4	Why do you want to work for TK Maxx?		400	
5	Why do you want to work in merchandising?		400	
6	Tell us about a time where you were responsible for a project		300	
7	Tell us about a time where you had to communicate an idea		400	
8	What are your interests?		300	

Don't be too romantic about choosing companies to apply to. The information on their websites is generic and you can't tell whether it's a good place to work simply by reading a few hundred words and watching some choreographed videos. There's no point being picky at this stage. Get them into your sheet quickly and efficiently so you can spend more time perfecting your application and interview technique.

To save time, our team at AcademicUnderdogs.com can do all of the above for you. We will:

1. Register a graduate or internship account with each of your target BIG organisations.

2. Enter all of your basic information to save you time.

3. Create and fill out your tracking sheet including all the application questions.

4. Edit and proof read your answers—send us a word vomit or some bullet points and we will turn it into perfectly written answers.

5. Work with you to improve your answers with unlimited revisions.

6. Provide access to GradGenius, a large database of psychometric practice tests.

7. Offer unlimited mentorship for a year from one of our specialist career advisors.

We can also:

1. Send LinkedIn enquiries and e-mails to hundreds of SMALL organisations on your behalf.

2. Follow up with each company up to 7 times or until you receive an interview.

3. Conduct mock interviews and tailored advice to help you convert interviews with small organisations into internships and job offers.

How to Find Small-Medium Size Companies

Look inside your personal network first—immediate family, peripheral family, friends, family friends, neighbours, school alumni. If you know someone who works in the area that you're interested in, your chances of converting that relationship into work experience are high. That is why investing your time into calling around is worth it and should be your first step.

Once you have completed that step then you should create online profiles on all the major platforms including LinkedIn, angel.co, internwise.co.uk and Shapr. Create your profile under the assumption that every recruiter will see it, which means you need to keep spelling mistakes to a minimum and be as professional and succinct as possible. We have more hints and tips on how to create winning online profiles on AcademicUnderdogs.com.

Whenever you find an organisation that suits your criteria, add them to your Excel sheet and contact someone in the senior leadership team. Most companies don't share this information on their website so your best bet is LinkedIn. Many companies have a LinkedIn page and you can see who works there. Typically, senior staff or founders of the company will state their rank, but you may need to do a little detective work to narrow down the options.

Helena: *"My mum knows someone who works as a buyer for an e-commerce retailer. I've reached out to him."*

Me: *"Good work! An early face-to-face meeting is important. Meet him for a coffee but make sure you go to him, don't ask him to come to you. Ask him pre-prepared questions about his career. Be honest and direct."*

Helena: *"OK, but apart from that lead, I've found it quite difficult to find other small-to-medium size companies that offer buyer internships."*

Me: *"Small companies generally don't advertise internships or actively hire graduates. However, that doesn't mean they won't take you on for a few weeks over the summer if you reach out to them. They may even create a job for you."*

Helena: *"What do you mean?"*

Me: *"One of my mentees, Nikhil, was interested in investment banking. He applied to a bunch of large companies all for the same position but also sent enquiries to 100+ smaller companies. Many of these companies had nothing to do with investment banking but they were all connected to finance in some way. One company that responded was a 1 year old FinTech company that built products for asset managers and banks. They weren't even thinking about hiring an intern, but Nikhil's e-mail did enough to impress and one of the founders decided to interview him."*

Me: *"The two founders openly told Nikhil that they were too busy building the company to train him and that he would have to add value wherever he could."*

Helena: *"Did he go for it?"*

Me: *"Yep! He first helped them set up their office in London and worked with an IT consultant to get the computers/network in place. A few weeks later he was sitting in on calls with customers, marketing agencies, software developers and investors."*

Helena: *"It doesn't sound like he was doing anything related to banking."*

Me: *"He wasn't. However, both of the employees were ex-investment bankers and he learnt a lot through observation. Over time he built a number of relationships with the bankers and they went out of their way to help him learn about the industry."*

Helena: *"What did he do next?"*

Me: *"They offered him a full-time job but Nikhil wanted to explore other areas of finance. He used the knowledge and experience he had acquired to secure an internship the following year."*

Helena: *"Amazing!"*

Me: *"With smaller companies, don't worry if they specifically have, or need, a retail buyer. Focus on the people running the company and what you could learn from them."*

Helena: *"How did Nikhil find that small company in the first place?"*

Me: *"Both founders were actively looking for various freelancers on Fiverr.com. Nikhil had done some freelance design work on Fiverr before and could see their requests. He reached out to them through the platform!"*

Helena: *"That's so creative!"*

Me: *"Yes, and there's no reason you can't do the same. From a quick search, I found a website called Trouva.com that helps small boutique retailers sell their products online. It has a list of 200 high street boutique retail stores that sell everything from clothes to furniture. You should put all those stores into your tracking sheet. Add Trouva.com in too!"*

Helena: *"I never thought of that, but surely reaching out to all of them will take ages."*

Me: *"It will, but that's what it takes to secure good work experience without much on your CV."*

academicunderdogs.com

PACKAGE 1 – TIME SAVER

You tell us:

- What industry, companies or jobs you're interested in.

- Basic information (university, age, date, etc).

We:

- Provide a shared job-tracking sheet to gather data and keep your organised.

- Start the applications on each graduate website by entering all of your basic information.

- Enter the application questions from each company into one Excel sheet for you to complete in your own time.

PACKAGE 2 – APPLICATION BOOSTER

Everything in package 1 AND

- Full edit and proofread of your answers by an experienced career advisor.

PACKAGE 3 – CAREER DOMINATOR

Everything in package 1 & 2 PLUS

- We will contact multiple small-medium sized companies on your behalf and follow up with them up to 7 times or until we get a response.

- Unlimited mentorship from one of our career advisors for 1 year.

- Full money back guarantee if you don't get an internship, job offer or work experience.

Identify Target Organisations and Build a Database

- Create a tracking sheet where you can build a database of employers and their application questions.

- Start by researching large companies in all the obvious places—Google, Milkround, Times Top 100 Graduate Employers.

- Register accounts on all the large companies and then copy & paste their key application questions into your tracking sheet.

- Search your personal network for start-ups and small companies.

- Use sites like Linkedin, Internwise and Angel.co to find other small companies in your target industry.

Helena: *"I've registered my details at 12 large companies that offer retail buyer internships, found 30+ smaller companies and filled out my tracking sheet"*

Me: *"Great! Do you see why it's best to get all this done first?"*

Helena: *"Yes, a lot of companies ask very similar questions like, 'Why do you want to work for us' and 'Demonstrate this & that skill'. I have a much better idea of the amount of time I need to write out all these answers and send applications."*

Me: *"It's always best to create a database of answers for these common competency questions as you will be asked them continuously by both small and large companies."*

Chapter 33
What's Your Truth-Blag Ratio?

"Are you a team player? Give me an example of when you worked in a team?"

"Have you ever worked with anyone difficult? How did you handle it?"

"Give me an example of where you used your communication skills."

These are all examples of competency questions. You'll be asked a lot of these in the foreseeable future, both in applications and interviews. Before creating your CV, you should write answers for all possible competency questions.

Try thinking of answers for the questions written above. Could you think of anything? Chances are you don't have answers for some of them and the ones you do have answers for are a little uninspiring. In this situation, most students do what they do best: Blag.

There is always going to be some exaggeration and curve fitting when filling out applications, but if you want the job then you need to keep that to a minimum.

Being truthful on your application significantly increases your chances of getting the job. The people tasked with reading those CVs and sorting the wheat from the chaff are pretty adept at knowing what's real, what's fake and what's shameless hyperbole. After all, they've read thousands of CVs before yours and they've interviewed the people who wrote them.

Your recruiters know that most people exaggerate. They've seen it before and there's a good chance they did it themselves as well. The cynical among them will be looking for any clue of deception. A slightly longer than average hesitation, change in voice pitch, flickering eye lash, tensed forehead or stutter caused by uncertainty in your own mind will set off alarm bells.

As you leave the interview room, they will collect their thoughts and feelings and then conclude that something wasn't right. Most of the time they won't even be able to articulate why, they'll just know that something was right.

Not only is it imperative that you tell the truth, but it's also important to backup these statements with real life examples where possible.

"I worked in a small restaurant part time for a little while. One evening, my new colleague made a mistake with an order and

the manager screamed at her. It wasn't even a big mistake. It seemed like he was venting frustrations from his personal life. Everyone fell silent, waiting for her to be sacked. In her defence, the order process was pretty challenging and it wasn't her fault.

I counted to 3 and then spoke up. I backed her up and presented a solution. Following my lead, another colleague chipped in, my boss calmed down and the conversation moved on.

Taking that risk, doing the right thing and speaking up paid off. All my colleagues treated me differently after that day and we built pretty strong relationships. I didn't work there long but we still speak to this day.

Eventually, someone else bought the restaurant and, after consulting all the staff, they made me assistant manager! They nominated me over others that had worked there longer just because I had the balls to stop an emotional tirade.

-    *Wil Ki*

It doesn't matter if your examples are not extraordinary. Sure, developing websites that name Chinese babies or climbing mount Everest will give you an edge, but using storytelling to display superior levels of emotional intelligence can be equally effective. Wilson's example above screams authenticity and EQ (emotional intelligence). We are all emotional beings at the end of the day and are drawn to people who understand and empathise with us.

It's also easy to spot a blag when you ask a follow-up question. Imagine that you're trying to impress a group of friends in a discussion about meeting famous people. They're all giving impressive answers and you realise that the closest you got to meeting someone famous was sitting in the front row of a Justin Bieber concert (something that no one wants to admit to in polite company). The conversation gets to you, you hesitate and in the spur of the moment you decide to blag it and tell them that you once had dinner with Beyonce.

You could probably commit to the lie for a little bit, but what happens when they start asking questions? The lie goes deeper, your hesitations become more pronounced, you start contradicting yourself, and it becomes obvious that you're lying.

An interviewer isn't going to care whether you shared a garlic bread with Queen B, but they will ask a lot of follow-up questions about any worthwhile statement that you make and if they detect a lie, those questions will keep coming.

"Give me an example of your leadership skills?"

"Was there anyone in your team that didn't pull their weight? How did you manage them?"

"Did they eventually get their work done?"

"Why do you think he didn't do it in the first place?"

If your story is true, you can answer these questions without hesitation. Not only will you have spoken about them before, but you'll also be drawing from your actual memory of these events. If you practice them, even better. By thinking of these questions beforehand you can prepare for them and ensure that your answers are prompt, succinct and professional, which is to say that they won't be filled with "uhms" and "ars" as you try to recall.

One interviewer asked me a bunch of these after I gave a real example on a design project I did with a group of people at uni. I stalled on some because I just hadn't thought about these questions before. I ended up going back to some of my team members and asking them questions like:

Me: *"You know when we did that design project? Remember that disagreement we had on week 2? Do you think I handled the situation properly or was I being a brat?"*

Ali: *"Look, it was the first time I spoke to you since we started this course and the first time we worked together. I did think you were a little abrupt and bossy, but that conversation completely changed my view of you. I'm glad you approached me to square things up and it's probably the reason we are mates now."*

In the very next assessment centre, one of the interviewers asked the same competency question about my team working skills and similar follow up questions about 'dealing with difficult team members'. This time, I didn't stutter and pretty much repeated what Ali said to me. The interviewer immediately complimented me on 'setting the record straight' with my team member for the greater good of the project and commended my initiative to ask Ali for feedback.

Put your Hand Up

Everyone blags and exaggerates in the beginning. When I first sent out applications, my truth-blag ratio was probably around 10%-90%. I quickly figured out that blagging was easy on applications but very difficult to do in interviews. I felt very uncomfortable lying to the extent I did and they could see it. That's why I went on a campaign to create real life examples.

Every time I spotted an opportunity to create a 'competency story', I jumped at it. In my final year at university, we were tasked with creating a design project that counted for a big chunk of our final grade. I went ahead and took the leadership position in the team, with the hope that a good competency answer would come from it.

From reading books on 'killer interview questions and answers', I saw an answer that said something like:

What's Your Truth-Blag Ratio?

"I spent some time looking at what was required to complete the project, set out a schedule of tasks, determined who should do what based on what they were good at and created a 'gantt chart'"

I literally copied what that guy did and presented my gantt chart to my team members in a casual/laid back way. They were completely taken aback and accepted me as a team leader.

Each of them knew the importance of the project and were happy to have someone take the reins and steer it towards completion. They knew that I would do whatever it took to secure the highest grade possible. I was essentially a project manager and team leader for 6 months.

Taking this simple step improved my leadership skills and won me at least 20 competency answers. What's more, whenever I handled a difficult situation, I wrote down every detail on my phone so that I wouldn't forget. Details show interviewers you are telling the truth. Those details continuously impressed during interviews that I had months later.

In an attempt to produce better interview answers, I actually ended up developing the competency skills that these employers wanted! During another assessment, I was placed in a group of 8 people and asked to come up with a solution to a problem. I spoke out first and organised everyone so that we would finish on time. It worked, I scored highest in the group and won a final round interview.

Use S-T-A-R

Situation, Target, Action and Result. Use this structure for all of your competency questions but always make sure your answers are explained as stories. Notice how Wil didn't say:

Situation: "My manager was angry at my colleague and was about to sack her."

Target: "I wanted to save her."

Action: "I stepped in and steered the conversation into positive territory and put forward a solution."

Result: "My manager responded positively, her job was saved and I improved one of the processes of the business."

In Wilson's interview answer, he used the STAR structure to form the answer, but told it as a story.

You can also vary the length of your answers. If you have a great answer with a high truth-blag ratio, tell it like a story to capture the interviewer's attention. For other examples where you've had to blag more, keep it shorter and more structured. That way you won't feel that you are talking too much and you'll be keeping the interviewer(s) engaged.

Write Down your Best Examples

Try answering the competency questions below using the truth and nothing but the truth. Create 3 answers for each question:

1. Teamwork: "Tell me about a time you led or worked in a team."

2. Problem Solving: "Describe a situation where you solved a problem."

3. Decision Making: "Give an example of a time where you made a difficult decision."

4. Leadership: "Describe a situation where you showed leadership."

5. Responsibility: "Tell me about a time you took re-sponsibility for a project."

6. Communication: "Tell me about a time you displayed good communication skills."

Most of the competency questions you will be asked in applications and interviews will either be these exact ones or a derivation of them.

What's your Truth-Blag Ratio?

Reduce your blagging over time by developing competency skills. Volunteer for stuff at uni and be more active during group tasks and discussion.

Look at good answers and emulate them in real life. This means putting your hand up to be project leader if your course has group work; putting yourself forward for leadership at a large university sponsored society; starting a business at university and growing it to the point where you can hire other undergrads to work for you. This is harder than joining a society or being team leader in a group project, but you will be rewarded dearly.

As you gain work experience, you will naturally find the answers to these examples. My second round of interviews were much easier after my internship.

In preparation for the interview, rehearse your examples in the mirror to improve your oral articulation. After a while the "ums" and "ahs" will disappear and you will communicate your examples clearly. This will leave you with more time and energy to focus on reading body language and using humour, thus influencing your interviewer more effectively.

Structured competency answers that project a repertoire of skills and emotional intelligence will give you a significant edge over other candidates.

Of the 9 candidates joining you at the final round assessment day, your superior competency answers will help you beat 6 of them. Beating the other 3 requires a little magic.

Chapter 34
What's Your X-Factor?

Imagine that you are in competition with 2 million people, all of which are in the same generation and geographical location and perform at the same academic level. Given that all of these people have been through a similar journey to you so far, how do you differentiate yourself?

It's easy to say to yourself, "I'm intelligent and skilled" or "I have had a hard life and have a lot of experience", but the same could be said for everyone else, or at least for the majority of them. It can be hard to look at yourself in relation to everyone else. We all believe that we're unique and that our skills, our intelligence and our understanding of the world is much better than our peers. This is especially true when we're young. But that simply isn't the case and the truth is that there are probably more capable people out there than you and many of these will be applying for the same jobs.

To stand out, you need to work a little harder on presenting yourself and your skills to the interviewers—as the saying goes, "Hard work beats talent when talent doesn't work". There are four areas that you need to focus on to make sure you stand out:

1. Creative ventures.

2. Sport.
3. Positions of responsibility.
4. Entrepreneurship.

Creative Ventures

Do you dance, sing, play an instrument, draw, paint, write or practice any other form of creative expression? Have you done this from a young age? If so, focusing on these over the next few years could help you stand out to employers. However, playing an electric violin beautifully in your bedroom or writing engaging short stories on a personal blog located on the 10th page on Google isn't enough.

Share your music on platforms like SoundCloud or YouTube and perform live. Send your novel to a publisher and your short stories to anthology creators and genre magazines. Record your street magic performances and organise viral flash mobs. Sign up to every competition or opportunity that provides a platform for you to share your creative expression with large audiences. This is how you leverage your interests and talents to help you secure a job. It will also boost your confidence and enhance your c-skills, as mentioned in the second book of this series, *How to be Admired & Respected.*

Think about how you can use your creative talent to add value to a large group of people. Your answer will probably involve stepping outside of your comfort zone in some way. Most won't have the courage to do so and that is why their CVs will fall to the bottom of the pack. By taking a chance and risking a little embarrassment that no one will remember, your recruiters will remember your name.

Sport

Sport is a fantastic way to stand out, but only if you compete at a high level. In my experience, it's usually too late to pick up a new sport after the age of 18 so this option is reserved for those who have continuously played from a young age.

Some of my mentees played multiple sports at a young age then focused on one over time. They usually continued playing well beyond school—first or second teams at university, company teams, weekend leagues or tournaments at district and county level.

The sacrifice and discipline required to compete at high levels is universally understood by most people, including your future employers. These will always give you an edge over other candidates so don't give up.

Positions of Responsibility

As the president of the Urban Music Society at UCL, which had a grand total of 10 members, I can confidently say that leading small societies will add no value to your CV whatsoever! Being elected to a position of responsibility for a large society, however, does help you stand out.

Believe it or not, most graduate recruiters know the difference between well-established university societies and the 'Micky Mouse' ones. Human resources at investment banks, for example, look favourably upon leaders (President, treasurer, etc.) in the most popular societies at top universities. These include the 'Business & Finance' group at the LSE and 'Economics & Finance' society at UCL.

Competition for the top spots at these societies is fierce. Recruiters know that you had to work hard and persuade many of your peers to secure a leadership position. Furthermore, managing society responsibilities alongside everything else will develop skills many of your fellow students don't have.

Positions of responsibility in organisations outside of university can also impress. If these aren't very well known, you may need to communicate the importance of them clearly to recruiters.

Entrepreneurship

Entrepreneurs have had a huge impact on society over the past decade. The likes of Steve Jobs, Mark Zuckerberg, Elon Musk, Jeff Bezos and a raft of other successful entrepreneurs have inspired the world. Interestingly, the older generation are looking to the younger ones for inspiration.

Technology is creating rapid disruption and change in all kinds of industries. Leaders understand they need to innovate quickly to prevent falling behind their competition. To do this, they need to hire well-rounded and creative people. Nothing screams 'innovative and creative' like a 19 or 20-year-old who has turned an idea into a revenue generating business.

As I mentioned in chapter 24, if you don't have an X-factor and are wondering how to compete with Oxbridge candidates, entrepreneurship is where you should be looking.

Do what your potential employers do on a smaller scale. Like Helena, if you want to go into retail, source products and sell them. If you want to be a software engineer, code software. If you want to be a marketer, market products.

If you don't have an idea, start with the obvious, easy and cheap. Write blogs, record podcasts, create YouTube videos, sell products on Amazon and eBay. Getting your feet wet with these 'gateway ventures' will develop your skills and generate better business ideas.

Six months after publishing *How to ACE Your A-Levels*, a student asked if I could come to their school to deliver workshops, and I obliged. A year later I was visiting schools up and down the country delivering workshops and rolling out mentorship programmes. It was a huge success. Recently, one customer suggested making a mobile application to help students learn bulky content—we're currently in the process of developing this platform. New and better ideas will come, but you need to start with something first.

What is Your X-factor?

Ten years ago, undergraduates didn't have to think about developing an X-factor beyond their academic study. Degrees impressed employers and having one would guarantee you a job. That is no longer the case.

With almost 400,000 graduates entering the workforce each year, supply has increased. Grade inflation is also a problem. Almost a third of students graduate from university with first class honours, the highest grade awarded by most universities.

What you do outside of university is becoming more important than what you do inside. Sports and creative ventures help you to stand out. However, extra-circulars that compliment your desired career path can add much more value. Innovative and scalable businesses are best, but smaller creative ventures can also add considerable value to your CV.

An X-factor is formed when your understanding of yourself and the world around you **significantly** exceeds that of your peers. Bottom line, to achieve this, you need to do things that those around you don't.

Helena: *"I play the piano but don't really have an X-factor—what should I do?"*

Me: *"I think you should start a retail business. Luckily, we live in a time where setting up your own shop is fairly easy. Source*

322

products and sell them online. Your goal should be to source and sell at least one product. Take it as seriously as you do your degree."

Helena followed my advice and set up her own boutique retail store focused on selling plant fibre products. She set up a shop on Shopify, Amazon and eBay and then sourced her products on AliBaba. Her store, Thelia, was generating around £100 a month at the time.

Chapter 35
Starter Questions

Me: *"Tell me about yourself."*

Helena: *"I'm in my second year studying Chemistry. I'm also the founder of Thelia, an online and offline store that sells plant fibre products and I was once a barista. I make a really good Latte!"*

When Helena and I first met, her elevator pitch was 150 words and used a lot of generic phrases like:

'I'm hard working'

'I am passionate'

Launching a side-business raised her social value and boosted her pitch. Once she trimmed it down and added some tongue and cheek, she left the interviewer wanting to know more.

Me: *"Why do you want to be a retail buyer?"*

Helena: *"I'm a product person and have been since I first started working in my dad's pharmacy. When I was 16, I negotiated the price of a sweat pad at a Pharmacy Trade show and* *the lady at the stand said I would be a good buyer! That's what sparked the idea. I love sourcing products and spend an abnormal amount of time walking through supermarkets and retail stores looking at every detail—the displays, stands, packaging, tags, materials and pricing. I was never a numbers person but, ever since I started Thelia, I've come to enjoy the business side too. Evaluating a product, making a judgement on whether it will sell and looking at the economics is fascinating."*

This answer consistently received positive feedback for Helena because every word is true. Her truth-blag ratio is 100-0 and her word choice conveyed a genuine interest in retail buying.

She subtly conveys a life-long interest in this career path without saying it outright. Mentioning a family member's influence projects humble down-to-earth qualities that anyone would find relatable. Remarks about buying underarm sweat pads at trade shows and spending abnormal amounts of time in retail stores shows passion in a tastefully humorous way.

She ends the answer with Thelia and this would be the second time she mentions it. This is no accident. Helena knows that everyone admires and respects those who take creative risks. She has plenty of detailed answers prepared for questions about her business.

Answers that show the interviewer both her technical knowledge and soft skills—revenue, gross margin, landed cost, duty, MOQ, VAT, these are all terms Helena will mention.

She's ready to talk through an example of how she evaluated a product and chose suppliers.

"I found two products that I loved. Both were children's dinner sets made from renewable bamboo fibre. Because of MOQs (minimum order quantities), I could only afford one of them. One had an incredible design but higher landed cost and, therefore, lower margin. The other design was OK but wasn't as good—it had a larger margin. After negotiating as much as possible with both suppliers, I decided to go with the latter one but with better packaging and market it in a different way on Amazon. The first one was tempting but it was risky and the economics didn't make sense at the time."

From her research and speaking to people in the industry, she knew that buyers have dilemmas like these all the time. The recruiter doesn't care if she made the right choice or not. They want to see a passionate individual who will add value. Helena's answer ticks both of these boxes.

Starter Questions

Your elevator pitch should change over time as you gain more experience and find better ways to explain who you are. Open up a notes section on your phone headed, 'Elevator pitch'. Over the next few years, you're going to hear certain phrases and words that describe you well. Note these down.

Chapter 36
How to Write an Attention-Grabbing CV

Most people write their CVs before creating answers for competency and starter questions. This never made sense to me because interviewers ask questions based on what's written on your CV. Doesn't it make more sense to create the answers to common interview questions first and then use those to build your CV?

Me: *"What's your favourite interview answer?"*

Helena: *"I've got a good example of when I demonstrated problem solving skills that also gets a laugh from people. It comes from back when I was working in my dad's pharmacy. There was an inventory issue and my dad thought his staff were stealing from him, but it turned out that there was an error with the supplier invoices. I diffused an argument between the staff and my dad, which was the funny anecdote, and then negotiated a discount with two of our suppliers."*

Me: *"Excellent. That should be bullet point 1 under the pharmacy experience in your CV."*

May '17 – Dec '18   Malvern Pharmacy (MP) Ltd – Retail Manager

- Collaborated closely with staff, suppliers and business owners to service a variety of local customers.

Helena's interviewers would have her CV printed out in front of them during interviews and they'll be drawn to this first bullet point:

Interviewer: 'How did you collaborate closely with staff, suppliers and business owners?'

Helena: 'My job was to manage the medicine inventory, as well as the staff and till machine. However, on a number of occasions, I had to step in to solve problems and conflicts between the staff.'

Interviewer: 'Tell me more about that.'

Helena: 'For example, there was one occasion where inventory was missing and a fight broke out between the owner and some of the staff...'

--

Interviewer: 'Tell me about a problem you solved during your time at the pharmacy.'

Helena: 'On one occasion, we found quite a few products missing from the back which resulted in a fight between one of the owners and the staff. Here's what happened...'

--

Interviewer: 'Did you ever have to deal with a difficult customer? How did you manage that?'

Helena: 'A few times, but the trickiest situation was when a fight broke out between one of the owners and staff. Here's what happened...'

Helena could deliver her favourite answer to a number of questions asked by the interviewer based on this bullet point. Through your CV, you can direct the interviewer's attention to topics and experiences that you enjoy talking about. Not all your interview answers and competency examples will be equally strong. Always look to bring your strongest answers forward in your CV.

Helena: *"How many pages should my CV be?"*

Me: *"It should never be more than 1 page and formatted correctly."*

Formatting

How to Write an Attention-Grabbing CV

Generous spacing, icons and a trimmed down minimal content can do wonders for your CV.

This is what you should be aiming for. Don't worry if your CV doesn't have as much content as the one above because it's from an exceptional mentee who was in his early 20s at the time. It's the formatting and layout that I wanted to draw your attention to.

Icons are commonly used by graphic designers and big companies in various forms of media. They look great on your CV.

These are currently available on a bunch of websites but I use fontello.com. Download the icons you want, save the .tff file as a font on your computer then copy/paste the icons from the demo.html into your word document.

Chapter 37
Asset Checklist

By the end of this process, you should have the following completed:

Answers to core competency questions (3 answers each)

1. 3 x Teamwork: "Tell me about a time you led or worked in a team."

2. 3 x Problem Solving: "Describe a situation where you solved a problem."

3. 3 x Decision Making: "Give an example of a time where you made a difficult decision."

4. 3 x Leadership: "Describe a situation where you showed good leadership skills."

5. 3 x Responsibility: "Tell me about a time you took responsibility for a project."

6. 3 x Communication: "Tell me about a time you had to communicate something difficult."

Starter Questions

7. Elevator Pitch: "Tell me about yourself."
8. Reasoning: "Why do you want to be in this career?"

Personal Branding

9. CV
10. LinkedIn & other online profiles

Once all your assets are in place, you can start filling in your online applications for the larger companies. Systematically make your way through your tracking sheet. Answering most of the applications will only require copy and pasting, the rest will most likely be industry specific or technical questions like:

"What challenges do you think the retail industry faces right now?"

Not all companies ask questions like this, but those that do usually ask different ones. I won't be able to provide general advice when answering these types of questions because each industry is different. This is where your industry mentors and resources will come in handy.

Your assets and answers should never be stagnant. As you become more aware of the skills your employers demand, jump out of your comfort zone continuously to generate better skills and stories.

Chapter 38

How to Secure a Job at a Small Company

Most large companies have a formal online application process followed by several rounds of assessment. They actively look for graduates to fill their annual quotas and they welcome applications. Securing a job at a small company, particularly those who aren't actively looking for interns or grads, requires a completely different process.

Getting your foot in the door at smaller companies will require a combination of networking and internet mass marketing. You need to become familiar with Linkedin, Angel.co and Internwise.co.uk. There will be a lot of people ignoring your e-mails and there will be many outright rejections as well, so try to remain emotionally detached and just keep hitting your daily targets.

After finding a few leads, message them using the InMessaging service or by upgrading to the Sales Navigator package. At the time of writing, there is a one month free trial that gives you 20 free messages. Start with this and upgrade when you are ready. Trust me—it's worth the money.

You won't be the only person using this tactic and this is why creativity matters. Recruiters see the same stuff every single day so even the slightest ingenuity and tasteful self-expression can prevent them from ignoring your e-mail. Here is an e-mail that landed me an interview and subsequent offer from a small company in London.

SUBJECT: For the attention of Daniel Ellis

Hi Daniel,

Having traded FOREX and built my own systematic trading system whilst at university, I have generated a return of 9% with a max draw-down of 3% over the past 6 months.

I have also written and attached a 60-page book summarising the key learning points from several Technical Analysis and Trading books. Please feel free to share it with your team.

Currently, I am studying Chemical Engineering at University College London and am on track for a First-Class Honours degree.

I'd be grateful if you could spare some time to speak with me over the phone. Please find my CV attached. I'm confident that I can add value to your team and Futex.

Thanks,
Anshul

My first few lines outline creative pursuits that differentiate me from everyone else. Mentioning my university, course, society work or anything else would risk Daniel losing interest and clicking 'delete'. I had to grasp his attention immediately.

Also, notice that the message is short and snappy. Cover letters targeting large corporations are usually fairly lengthy, but people are much more likely to respond to shorter messages on social platforms and e-mail. Hyperlinks and attachments help reduce word count. I hyperlinked the phrases 'systematic trading system' and '60-page book' to my own web domain (anshulraja.co.uk). Anyone reading my e-mail had the option to click through and read further details about my creative pursuits. Daniel later said:

"Look, I thought your trading system was awful. However, I'd never seen a grad take the effort to create a web page and present themselves in the way you did. Did you really write that book?"

Writing that short book took about 30 hours. By sending this to senior managers, I was already trying to add value to their company before even being employed. Even if the book didn't help, they could see I was a self-starter and was enthusiastic enough about the industry to create my own resource. Well thought out creative pursuits always impress more than good grades.

Through tracking, I could see that every single person who opened my e-mail also clicked through to my website. Google analytics showed how long they spent on each page. If someone clicked onto my website several times, I'd send them more information about me and follow up with phone calls.

Moving the conversation away from e-mail or LinkedIn and onto phone or face-to-face is crucial. You can't express your tonality via words on a screen. Even if you have a squeaky annoying voice, the chances of landing an interview increase if you can get on a call. As an introvert, I found e-mailing much more comfortable than calling but eventually formed a habit to pick up the phone. There is no room for shyness and social anxiety when finding a job. You have to reach out to people and speak with confidence and purpose even if you're nervous inside.

Helena: *"So create online profiles and start with short e-mails/LinkedIn messages?"*

Me: *"Spot on."*

Helena: *"Should I keep e-mailing and messaging people until I receive a response?"*

Me: *"Essentially yes, but you need to be careful that you don't overdo it. Follow up with a second e-mail or phone call after 3 business days. After 5 or 6 attempts without a response, move on to other leads."*

Helena: *"Should I contact people on weekends?"*

Me: *"No. A study conducted by GetResponse analysed 21 million messages and showed that the best open and response times were between 8AM – 10AM and 3PM – 4PM on weekdays. Sending e-mails between 2 – 3PM always worked better for me."*

Helena: *"Can you help me put together draft messages?"*

Helena and I drafted a first engagement e-mail below:

How to Land Your Dream Graduate Job

SUBJECT: For the attention of ...

Dear ....,

Having built a retail business selling plant fibre products while at university, I have developed a range of skills that may be valuable to .... I'm a second-year undergraduate and I'd like the opportunity to work for you.

..... is a great company with a strong mission that resonates with me on a personal level. I'm interested in a career in retail and would like to join your team for a few weeks this summer.

I have strong relationships with several plant fibre suppliers in China and an excellent understanding of this market. During a summer internship at your company, I'd be delighted to launch a range of garments made from real bamboo and seaweed fibre. I'm confident that these sustainable products can generate additional profits for you at a relatively low risk.

If you're interested, I'm available to speak over the phone or face-to-face during evenings, weekends and the following times:

22nd October : 12:00 – 15:00
23rd October : 10:00 – 12:00
26th October : 13:00 – 14:00
29th October : 15:00 – 17:00

Please find my CV attached and thank you for your consideration.

Thanks,
Helena

This e-mail received an enthusiastic response from the CEO of a small online clothing retailer. Helena received an offer after two interviews. In the final interview, the CEO offered her a position under the women's clothing buyer and a small budget to launch a plant fibre product on their website. Helena was told to work on her product as a project in addition to her main duties during the internship!

Again, most of the value comes from her X-factor. If she sent an enquiry with the usual spiel about how passionate and hard-working she was, would it have received the same response, or even a response at all? I doubt it. All small business owners want to hire competent people and are always looking for a cheap, low-risk way of increasing their revenue. Present both of those on a platter and the recruiter will probably bite.

What if you don't have an X-factor yet? Preempt problems your target companies have, or ways to increase their profits, and find a creative way to help them. Some of my mentees have asked younger employees about the issues at their companies and sent reports on how they can help solve them to the senior leadership team.

Managing Leads

Helena was lucky to receive an interview let alone an offer from her first few enquiries. As a rule of thumb, 4/5 enquiries will not receive any response and the rest will result in:

1. Yes, I'll interview you (Red—hot lead).
2. Maybe, try back another time (Orange—warm lead).
3. No, we're not looking for an intern right now (Blue —cold lead).

Colour code your tracking sheet so you can see the high probability leads at a glance:

Small Companies

Lead strength	Organisation name	Contact
	Kelly Group	N/A
	KiKi Wiki	Selena Khan
	Elisium Ltd	Harry Jiles
	Bella	Jake Lawson
	Selly Kellins LLC	Nik
	Cammy	Priya Shah

On several occasions, I e-mailed back my hot and warm leads a year later telling them about any new experiences I had. If you're getting consistent blues, you may need to tweak your email.

How to Secure a Job at a Small Company

Draft captivating e-mails and instant messages that small business owners can't ignore by:

1. Highlighting a real or potential problem they have in their business and suggesting how you can help them solve it.

2. Ask for an internship or job directly.

3. Mention your X-factor or any creative ventures first before anything else.

4. Create profiles and use instant messaging services on sites like Shapr, Linkedin, Angel.co, Crunchbase.com and Internwise.

5. Use services like those offered by my company academicunderdogs.com to contact small companies on your behalf.

Send e-mails and instant messages to all contacts on your tracking sheet. Any positive responses should be colour coded red to represent a hot lead which you should follow up aggressively. Orange and blue should be used for 'Maybe's' and 'No's' respectively.

Chapter 39
Big Companies

Each year, thousands of graduates apply to internship and graduate programmes at large well-known brands. There is a lot of competition!

Helena: *"This internship has 50 applicants per position, should I still go for it?"*

When I first stepped into the graduate job arena and the HR representative told me the number of people I was competing with, my immediate reaction was 'why bother?'. Why invest all this time when I only have a 1 in 50 chance of landing the job?

Hearing these stats made it seem like finding a job was impossible when it wasn't. It's true that some highly competitive industries receive multiple applicants per position. However, by following a solid strategy and honing your skills, you'll only be in competition with a handful of those individuals.

In a pool of 50 applicants at least half will offer little to no value, several more will be too anxious to get their benefits across and others will be too ill-prepared and inexperienced to capture the attention of the interviewers.

I realised this by the time I entered the second round. I knew I only really in competition with 10-15 applicants and that made the process much less daunting.

In my final year, I applied to around 12 companies and received offers from 4. One of those offers came from an investment bank that initially rejected me. After telling them about my other offers, they changed their tune and immediately sent me a contract.

You are in control of your own odds. Don't overestimate the quality of your competition or underestimate your own ability. As you become familiar with the recruitment process and hone your social skills, your odds will improve exponentially.

Application Process

Most large organisations recruit graduates every year and they make the application process relatively easy for you. They advertise on key publications and websites and they attend career fairs. Their application processes generally follow a similar pattern:

1. Online application
   a. Submission of CV and/or covering letter.
   b. Competency and/or technical questions.

2. Psychometrics tests, usually verbal and numerical reasoning.

3. Telephone competency interview with HR to check that you're a 'young adult' and not a 'frightened kid'.

4. First & final round assessment centre
   a. Series of competency and technical interviews.
   b. Case-study exercises.
   c. Team exercises.
   d. Role-play exercises.

All of this will seem daunting at first. However, once you've experienced the process from application to final round, you will feel much more confident. I nervously mumbled and fumbled my way through the first few interviews, so I know how it feels. Being judged so intensely isn't easy, especially if you've never been under a microscope before. But you will get used to it and may even begin to enjoy it.

Chapter 40
Acing Psychometric Tests

There is a fundamental flaw in psychometric testing and IQ testing; it is such a flaw that even Marilyn Vos Savant (the world's most intelligent woman) and Christopher Hirata (the world's most intelligent man) agree with this statement because you can quite easily practice psychometric tests and IQ tests to get better scores. You can use this flaw to your advantage and start maximising your psychometric test scores.

Employers Believe in Psychometric Tests

If people can practice and improve, then why isn't everybody doing it? The reason is twofold. Firstly, people don't commit to practicing and secondly, people have very ingrained feelings about psychometric tests that are almost as unshakable as their feelings about lie detectors.

The truth is that lie detectors work because they recognise our typically involuntary reactions and a regular Joe cannot beat a lie detector. However, people can be trained to fool lie detectors. This type of training is difficult, such as learning to convince yourself that you are so cold that your body starts involuntarily shaking to warm up. Yet, despite the fact that tests can be beaten, people still use them and rely on them. The same is true about psychometric tests, which means you can learn to beat them and come out on top. Practicing test questions over and over is enough to start bumping up your psychometric test scores.

Where to Find Adequate Practice Tests

Jump on Google to find a few recent practice tests. If they want you to sign up or pay, then skip and find another. If they want you to sign up and it looks good, use a disposable email address because they will sell your details to spammers.

The WikiJob website has a few practice tests. Skip to near the bottom of the page where they offer six, free psychometric tests. The tests are powered by Jobtestprep.co.uk which charges for tests.

Do not sign up for free trials because they all roll over into paid subscriptions that are very difficult to get out of.

PWC offers free tests and you can access a bunch of these on their site. If you get a chance, you should also take a look at their tips for preparing for psychometric tests.

Google the phrase 'psychometric test screenshots' and then click on Google Images. You will find hundreds of test questions you can try, and each image often leads to other suggested images. You can click on these to find the websites that originally posted the tests.

Hacks for Maximising your Psychometric Test Scores

For starters, become part of the online prepping community. This is where you post your screenshots, screen casts, and test answers for other people to use. Doing this will help draw viewers and 'likes' to your web pages and your social media profiles as mentioned earlier.

Google the tests you are due to take. Start with the name and look for what people have posted on their blogs. Check Google images too because it often shows direct screenshots of tests that people have copied and published.

Try to Google different titles, numerous times with different elements of your test. For example, you may Google the name of the test giver, or the codes written on the test, or the level of the test. It may have a reference code that you can search for. If other people have used these codes/names when posting their answers online, you will find them on the regular Google results or on Google images.

Some online psychometric tests have screen-cast blockers, but you should try to screen-cast/screen record the test anyway so you can analyse your answers and better prepare for the next test.

You can quickly screenshot your view on a Windows computer by holding down the Windows key (four squares on the bottom left of your keyboard) and the "PRTSC" key that is usually near the top right of your keyboard. The images will be automatically saved in your "Pictures" folder under "Screenshots" or "Saved Pictures" or "Camera Roll." If you're using a Mac, hit "CMD", "Shift" and "4" and then drag the box over the screen.

Strike deals with other people who are taking the tests. Ask them to take screenshots and send them to you. This is a common trick with co-workers who are taking appraisal tests. The hardest part is finding somebody you can trust.

Practicing Verbal Reasoning Tests

Read two or three paragraphs aloud, and then summarise what you have read without repeating what was written verbatim. Some teachers say you should put it in your own words, but that doesn't really cover what you are supposed to do. You need to show that you understand the main concept/point of what you have read.

Find the main point or concept that is written within the text you just read, and then describe the concept or point. It is less about summarising the writing and more about summarising the main point/concept and showing that you understand it. Try reading a variety of different texts so that you are not caught off guard. Try business-related material, a few paragraphs of fiction and even a bit of poetry.

If you are dyslexic or have a similar condition that may slow you down or impede you in some way, make sure you mention it to the test giver. As mentioned earlier in the "extreme responses answers" section, there are many unacceptable reasons to deny people a job, which means they cannot mark you down for having dyslexia, or a visual problem, etc. This also means you may be eligible for extra time/help which you will not be penalised for.

Some people practice by reading segments of the news; this is fine in moderation, but many news articles have a very simplified way of writing and reporting which isn't always suitable for practicing psychometric tests. News articles are more about shock and sensitisation, which means the points are often very basic and obvious. The same is often true of social media posts, so try to mix it up.

Practicing Numerical Reasoning Tests

You can use the Google Images method mentioned earlier to prepare for numerical reasoning tests. Almost all tests include large numbers that deal with millions/billions and convert them into different metrics, so it's a good idea to practice those.

Try free GCSE testing websites that show you data in different formats, such as graphs, charts and tables. Reacquaint yourself with these formats because they will probably appear in your tests. Answering a few GCSE questions will get you back into the swing of things.

When you see a question, take a few seconds to interpret the data yourself before you read the author's or the source's interpretations. Quite often, whatever pattern you are supposed to notice is more obvious prior to the issue being blurred by the question, or the source's interpretation.

You will probably be asked to identify trends in a chart or graph and you will probably be asked to calculate ratios, fractions and percentages. Many psychometric tests require you to perform multiple calculations in order to reach an answer. Also, many psychometric tests contain questions where you have to process numbers, such as turning percentages into decimals, or where you have to convert one metric to another, such as tonnes to kilograms.

Acing Psychometric Tests

The most powerful advice I can give you is to practice different test questions because it's the only consistent way to improve your psychometric tests scores. You should also be careful what you believe when you read advice about psychometric tests online because most writers have no idea how to improve psychometric tests scores and are simply rewriting what they have read online. Practice by whatever means you can and soon you will be an expert on taking psychometric tests.

Chapter 41
Interview Technique

Helena: *"I had my first interview last week."*

Me: *"How did it go?"*

Helena: *"It went OK..."*

Me: *"Go on..."*

Helena: *"I was a bit nervous to be honest and I think they saw that."*

Most of your examples present your skills in a clear and structured way. However, when an interviewer reads between the lines, they can see an array of other skills and a degree of emotional intelligence.

Your examples do most of the work for you. In culinary terms, they form the ingredients, recipe and the actual cooking process. All you need to do in the interview is present your delicious attributes in the best way possible.

Several factors can prevent you from doing this, including internal distractions and anxiety. Interviews are nerve-racking experiences, particularly if you haven't been through a 'proper' one before.

You may assume that they deal with nervous applicants all the time and that they can look past this, but that isn't necessarily the case. Think about the last time you spoke with someone who was a nervous wreck. How awkward did it make you feel, how did it impact the atmosphere of the room? Some interviewers will empathise, but many will find it hard to look past a lack of confidence. Put yourselves in their shoes. If you interviewed 10 grads in a day and 3 were nervous wrecks, wouldn't you focus on the other 7?

Furthermore, no one wants to work with someone who is a nervous wreck all the time. If you can't get it together during the interview they'll assume that's how you'll be on the job.

Obviously, you can't control your nerves simply by willing them to go away. But your nerves will settle the more interviews you have. If you take a look at my book, *How to be Admired & Respected* you'll learn some tips and techniques to stay calm and self-assured during the tensest of situations. If you don't have the book, here's a top-level break down of how to manage your external and internal distractions.

Reducing External Distractions

Your body is constantly emitting clues about your thoughts and feelings. Noisy background clatter in a coffee shop causes furrowed brows and tension to appear on your forehead. Tight clothing restricts breathing and raises the pitch of your voice slightly. Every time you move your arm, sweaty armpits trigger slight delays in your reactions to a conversation partner's comments. Non-verbal language effects your charisma.

Unfortunately, your interviewers won't know what's causing your corrupted body language. They will accept whatever you project and assume your discomfort is caused by them or something in your present situation. It will also distract them from all the positive body language signals and excellent examples you've spent weeks preparing.

Consciously controlling these signals is impossible. Prior preparation and an awareness of the effect that external distractions have on you is the only answer. It's easy to forget the obvious:

1.　Use adequate antiperspirant or other protection.
2.　Organise meetings in low noise venues where you can book tables.
3.　Wear comfortable clothing.
4.　Pick interview dates during comfortable periods of the month (for girls).
5.　Use talcum powder.
6.　Leave your house early.

Don't forget the basics!

Reducing Internal Distractions

From 'power posing' to '10 interactions', there are several techniques you can use to reduce anxiety during interviews. Here's a breakdown of all the top techniques:

1. 10 Interactions: Speak to a minimum of 10 people before your interview.

Before stepping foot into an interviewer's office, I would speak to or interact with 10 or more people. I would engage in small talk with the man queuing next to me for the bus; smile at the TFL (Transport for London) staff; start a conversation with a newsagent when buying a bottle of water; and chat with other candidates in interview waiting room.

Talking to people gets your social juices flowing and reduces anxiety. This is how you avoid early mistakes, like fumbling your greeting/handshake, and make a strong first impression. If you spend a lot of time on your own and in silence, you'll understand just how important this can be. The longer you're in those situations, the stranger you will feel when you make your first human interaction and the more anxiety you will exude. This is why you feel more comfortable toward the end of a conversation than you do at the beginning.

2.   Power Posing: Your body language changes your hormones.

Amy Cuddy, a social scientist from the USA, discovered that holding 'high power poses' for a few minutes increases testosterone and reduces cortisol levels in your brain. Stand with your arms out or on your hips with your head held high for 3-5 minutes in a toilet cubicle or other private space before the interview. This will have an immediate effect on your mood and confidence.

3.   ANT: Acknowledge, Neutralise & Transform.

Internal distractions are often caused by the same insecurities and anxious thoughts. I really want this job, what if I mess it up? What if I can't answer a question? You can't stop them from entering your head, but you can process them in a way that dampens their effects on your confidence. ANT, a variation of CBT (Cognitive Behaviour Therapy), is a good way to diffuse negative thoughts.

4.   Success Compilation: Watching videos of your past accomplishments.

As with power posing, watching or listening to relatable and inspiring content can also change your hormone levels. Watching a short video compilation of your past achievements and encouraging words from family members can do wonders for your confidence.

5.   Face Splash.

Evolution has gifted us with a 'Mammalian Diving Response', which causes our heart rate to slow when our skin comes in contact with water. This is why people splash their face with water when they are under stress—it works!

All of the above techniques are outlined in greater detail within the second book of this series, *How to be Admired & Respected.* These can be used in the weeks, days and minutes leading up to your interview.

Helena: *"I also felt a little awkward in the interview and felt the interviewer was dozing off."*

Me: *"You can use your body language to project more enthu-siasm. Also, sometimes you need to surprise or shock your in-terviewer with an unexpected answer or use humour to keep them interested. They probably interview every day and find it boring—be the candidate who is interestingly good and easy to talk to."*

Lean In

This technique was taught to me by Shamil Thakrar, a Harvard MBA and founder of the hugely successful restaurant chain Dishoom. Working at Goldman Sachs at the time, he said:

"Lean forward and open your eyes when emphasising your de-sire to work for your employer."

It worked a treat the first time I used it; I could tell by the inter-viewer's reaction. In subsequent interviews, I naturally as-sumed this 'lean forward' posture throughout the session as it felt more natural.

My career advisor always told me to keep my back against my chair, neck in neutral position and hands on laps. I followed their advice but always thought I looked a bit 'stuck up'. The 'lean forward' posture projected more desire and helped me speak with more energy and purpose. Have a go and see if it helps!

Raw Honesty

One of the most important tools you can have in your toolbox is surprising your interviewer with raw unapologetic honesty. From speaking to hundreds of successful graduates who have secured jobs, I've learned that going against conventional wis-dom and answering honestly, even if it feels uncomfortable, can pay off.

Rajesh, a close friend of mine, was rejected by dozens of bank-ing and finance firms after first-round interviews. Anticipating another rejection and out of frustration, in an interview with PWC, he responded to one question with raw honesty:

Interviewer: *"Why did you go to UCL."*

Rajesh: *"Because I was rejected by LSE."*

To Raj's surprise, the interviewer burst out laughing. He loved his answer. Most undergrads would have said something like:

"UCL has a great reputation and consistently tops world rankings. It also has a diverse student population with many students coming from outside the UK. I wanted to get to know people from different cultures and, as cliché as it sounds, broaden my horizons a little."

According to conventional wisdom the above answer is best, so why did Raj's answer win him an internship offer? Raw honesty projects confidence, security and authenticity. Interviewers hear the same answers continuously, so a candid undergrad is a breath of fresh air and an immediate green flag. Here's another example:

Interviewer: *"Give me an outline of your past positions of responsibility."*

Interviewee: *"I haven't had any real responsibility yet, but I see no reason why I'm not ready for it."*

Most interviewees would talk about a non-interesting position of responsibility for 10 minutes and state how well they did. If you don't have a good answer, a candid answer like the one above may be better. You wouldn't be able to get away with this if you were older than 25 years of age. However, as an undergraduate with limited work experience, interviewers will understand your position and respect your candour.

Humour

I was once interviewed by a team of 5 developers and there was a conversation with one of them that went like this:

Interviewer: *"What do you do when someone estimates a deadline that's too short for a project you're going to be working on?"*

Me: *"It really depends on the size of the project and how soon the deadline is. For example, if someone is asking me to build Facebook in 2 days, I'll probably let them know that it's not going to be feasible."*

They laughed a little on the Facebook example, which helped setting up the mood. Then he continued:

Interviewer: *"What if you were assigned a project that wasn't as large as Facebook, instead, a project that was small sized but with a tough deadline?"*

Me: *"In that case, I will inform them of my concerns and make sure I give them frequent updates about the progress. For instance, I'd report after 25% of the project time elapses how close am I to getting the project 25% done and so on. If* *it's getting closer to the deadline date and I haven't hit appropriate milestones I'd inform them that we are probably not going to be able to meet the deadline and we should consider extending it."*

Interviewer: *"What if they said that they're not going to be able to stretch the deadline date?"*

Me: *"Well... then I go Beast Mode and work late until I get it done."*

The entire room laughed really hard, I think most of the developers were gamers, so that resonated well. I ended up being hired.

Faisal Mudhir's answer on Quora (above) shows how effective humour is when building rapport with others. He gave a productive answer on his time management skills whilst also getting several laughs from his interviewers. Interactions like these can win the day!

Push-Pull

In *How to be Admired & Respected*, I define charisma as the balance of affection and authority. Both your verbal and non-verbal language projects these two qualities. For example, complimenting the interviewer's tie is an example of affectionate behaviour. A firm handshake is authoritative body language.

Project too much authority and you may come across as arrogant. An excessive amount of affection will make you seem desperate, needy and disingenuous. Knowing when you're veering off in one direction or the other takes practice. Once this becomes instinctive, you will naturally start 'pushing and pulling' your behaviour to maintain a balance. For example:

Push: "…as a result, I increased the ticket sales for my society by 50%"

Pull: "…which was great until we found out the comedy show lacked a key ingredient…comedy!"

Interview Technique

Employers often say they are looking for one thing when they are actually looking for something else. A lot of employers say they are looking for a candidate that has 'it'. An X-factor. When you ask them to articulate what 'it' is, they struggle and say 'it's instinctive—something I can just tell when speaking to them'.

'It' is a collection of data points collected by the interviewer by listening to what you say and reading between the lines.

Nailing interviews requires adequate preparation of your answers, managing both external and internal distractions and using unconventional methods to project charisma.

Chapter 42
Fire

Helena: *"I got an offer!"*

Me: *"Excellent! How do you feel?"*

Helena: *"Excited, nervous…I don't know!"*

Me: *"Who is it from?"*

Helena: *"An e-commerce startup selling pharmaceutical products online."*

Me: *"Are they paying you?"*

Helena: *"Yes, they raised their first round of funding a few months ago and are growing."*

If you haven't had much work experience before, this is exactly the type of opportunity you should aim for. Startups that secure funding are usually run by a small competent team of people who you can learn from.

Helena: *"What should I do now? Stop applying?"*

Me: *"Absolutely not! This gives you huge leverage in your job search. After receiving two offers from competing companies, I turned a rejection into an offer by simply calling them and telling them. If you have any 'warm leads' tell them about this offer. Keep applying to larger company internships too. 6 weeks at this startup followed by another 6 weeks at a larger company would equate to a very successful summer!"*

Several weeks later, after completing an assessment centre, Helena received a 10-month placement at a large retailer. After asking nicely, Helena's university deferred her final year to accommodate the placement. This is what you call a 'home run' in the graduate job world. Here's a reminder of how she did it and how you should too:

1. Use your self-stack sheet and extensive research to identify target organisations.

2. Create answers to common competency questions such as, 'Tell me about a time you demonstrated good communication skills?'.

3. If you find yourself 'blagging' answers, step outside your comfort zone in your day-to-day life to build skills that result in better answers.

4. Create your own X-factor by focusing on sport, creative ventures or entrepreneurship.

5. Create and continuously refine 'starter questions', such as, 'Tell me about yourself'.

6. Use answers to both competency and starter questions to create a 1-page CV and online profiles.

7. Systematically apply to large companies using online services to save you time (check out academicunder-dogs.com).

8. Persistently send enquiries to smaller companies using e-mail, direct messaging and calls (checkout academicunderdogs.com).

9. Practice psychometric tests and record live tests using screen recording software.

10. Before interviews, reduce both internal and external distractions using:

    a. 10 Interactions
    b. Power Posing
    c. ANT: Acknowledge, Neutralise and Transform.
    d. Success Compilation.
    e. Face Splash.

11. Use humour, lean in and push-pull during interviews to put yourself at ease and project charisma.

Step 4: Check

Chapter 43
Learn & Pivot

Helena received two more placement offers but decided to stick with the first one. We stayed in touch over the summer during both of her placements and caught up before she started her third year of university:

Me: *"Now that you've finished both of your internships, what are your thoughts for the future?"*

Helena: *"Both experiences were great and I received a full-time offer on the retail graduate programme starting next year!"*

Me: *"Congratulations!"*

Helena: *"Thanks! One of the founders from the start-up has said there should be a place for me there after graduating, but they can't commit just yet."*

Me: *"That's understandable given their size, but I'd still stay in touch with them periodically throughout the year."*

Helena: *"Yep. I definitely want to stay in retail and really enjoy the business side of the job."*

Me: *"Working with numbers and spreadsheets!?"*

Helena: *"Yes! I was worried about the numbers aspect of the role but I'm surprisingly good at it. There were several occasions during both internships where I had to calculate certain metrics for my manager and I got it right."*

Me: *"Did you ask your superiors for feedback?"*

Helena: *"Yes, several times, as you suggested. That's another reason why I think it might be an outlier skill. Both my managers said I had a knack for analysis and that my thought process was very entrepreneurial. These are the main changes I've made to my skills-stack sheet."*

Me: *"So I take it that law is not on your radar anymore?"*

Helena: *"I haven't thought about law for a while. In the near-term, I feel retail buying at an e-commerce company would be an ideal job for me. A job that meshes the best parts of both internships."*

Me: *"You have a lot more conviction in your voice than last year."*

Helena: *"Yes, things are much clearer now! In a buying role, I'll learn how to appraise products more effectively and pick winners. There is nothing stopping me from growing my side* *business simultaneously too. I like how both my business and career are closely related. The skills I develop from one helps the other. My parents agree with all this too!"*

The 'Win-Win' Position

Helena had an inkling that she was an undercover spreadsheet geek who enjoyed analysis, but she needed work experience and someone else to confirm this. Both her managers did just that. This is what your first few real experiences in the working world can do for you.

Dive headfirst into a fast-paced high growth environment with competent people. When you emerge from the other side your outlier skills will reveal themselves and the future will become more certain. You'll have a much better idea of what you want to do with your life. It only takes a few experiences to help you realise what you're good at and the type of work you will intrinsically enjoy.

Helena was in a great position with an offer in the bag and 12 months to take a few calculated risks. She could use her enhanced interest in retail to start a new business or focus on growing her current one. Using her updated skills-stack sheet, she could apply to other larger firms or enquire at innovative/disruptive smaller companies. She could also completely change her track and secure experience in a completely different industry to uncover more outlier skills. The choice was hers.

Surprisingly, after speaking to a patent attorney from the US, law came back into the picture a few months later. Helena spent a few weeks exploring law in detail and shadowed a few qualified lawyers at a small company to get a feel for the career. She ultimately went back to the world of retail and accepted her graduate job offer.

Helena may come across as indecisive and haphazard. As a graduate career advisor and coach, I can tell you that using this approach is smart. It becomes so much easier to experiment with various career ideas when you have an offer in the bag.

The most successful graduates get themselves into win-win situations. Remember Jacob, the founder of City Stasher? He focused intensely on building his business after securing a graduate job offer from a London bank. Jacob even tried to defer his start date by a year to give himself additional time to work on City Stasher. This is exactly how you should play the game.

Ticking all 3-Boxes

Even after starting her new permanent position, Helena never stopped her job search and continued to reach out to companies of all sizes. Almost a year after starting, she discovered a fashion and apparel e-commerce company that promoted positive body image. They weren't actively hiring but Helena knew that she'd be a perfect fit.

Just as she'd done hundreds of times over the previous 2 years, Helena sent an attention-grabbing and well communicated e-mail to the CEO asking to meet face-to-face. She had work-experience, interview experience and a top brand name on her CV. By leveraging all of this, she secured a full-time offer at the company within two weeks.

Learn and Pivot

When you land yourself an internship or job, focus entirely on adding value to your team and company. This is what your mantra should be throughout your internship. Every single day you walk into your place of work, your objective should be to make your manager and team's life easier.

"What do you think my strengths and weaknesses are?"

"What task did I perform best/worst in?"

"Do you think I have the right skills for this job?"

These are the type of questions you should be asking your man-ager. It helps to have critical superiors at a young age. My first ever manager called me out on a few of my flaws and it hurt at the time! I wept myself to sleep after one particularly gruelling day, but her feedback significantly helped me improve. In hind-sight, it was a blessing in disguise.

Periodically ask for detailed feedback from those closest to you and take their comments on board. After a few months, take some time to introspectively analyse your performance and update your skills-stack sheet accordingly.

Chapter 44
The Ultimate Graduate Job Strategy

Finding the right career is an iterative process that can last several years. Some people are lucky and find themselves in careers that fulfil them, while others live their whole lives not finding a well-suited career before eventually settling for something that doesn't make them happy. You create your own luck and nothing good comes out of sleepwalking through life. Picking a sound strategy and taking action will get you what you want. The P-A-F-C strategy worked for me and countless other's I've mentored.

Step1: Pick your Weapon

- Do you have quality work experience and/or conviction in a particular career path? Take a sniper approach and focus on a single industry or type of job.

- Nothing on your CV? Take a shotgun approach by starting your own business and/or enquiring at small companies.

- Are you nearing the end of your time at university? Use a hybrid approach, applying to both large and small organisations.

Step 2: Aim

- Research multiple industries and jobs to eliminate the obvious.

- Identify target organisations and create career-stack sheets.

- Narrow your options down to one or two career paths.

Step 3: Fire

- Create your assets by first writing down answers to common interview questions and then creating your CV.

- Systematically complete applications and use websites that save you time and help consolidate information.

- Reduce interview anxiety by using 10-interactions, ANT, success compilations and face splash.

- Use humour, raw honesty and push-pull during interviewers to project charisma.

Step 4: Check

- During your internship or work experience, focus on adding value to your team and organisation.

- Periodically ask for detailed feedback from your manager and team members.

- Update your skills-stack sheet and go back to step 4 and pivot if necessary.

- Keep looking for new and better opportunities.

- If all the ducks line up, don't be afraid to jump ship.

It is so easy to become narrow-minded in this process. If you leave things too late, panic sets in and you start choosing career paths based on your chances of getting in. Talks of finding jobs that have an impact on society or are suited to your skills go out of the window and fear of falling behind take over. You become emotional and ignore the evidence.

By starting early and following this process, you will avoid all these pitfalls and land your dream graduate job.

Onwards & Upwards

Chapter 45

How to Land Your Dream Graduate Job

Helena: *"I just don't know if I'm making the right choices. Nothing is certain and I'm anxious about the future."*

One of the most common causes of distress I hear from undergraduates and graduates is the fear of making the wrong choice. It's important to accept that you can't connect the dots going forward, and need to have faith in yourself and the process. No one goes from A to B without any hiccups. Everyone zigzags their way towards a fulfilling career and a fulfilling life. Failure is not only OK, it's necessary.

Don't worry about what everyone else is doing. In a state of anxiety, it's easy to be swayed by the words and actions of others. Finding a fulfilling career is simple but not easy. There will be rejections, and they will hurt, but it will get easier. Trust me on this one! Somewhere along the line, as long as you stick to the key principles outlined in this book, you will find success.

You may find glory in 3 years, 5 years or 10 years. You can't predict when it will come but you need to embrace the uncertainty and know that it will happen eventually.

At the start of the book, I mentioned the following:

21.3% of those survey in the Understanding Society UK Household Longitudinal Study said they were not satisfied with their work. Also, of the 79.7% who felt positively about their jobs, only 17.2% said they were completely satisfied.
   -   Office for National Statistics

Presented in this book, is a logical process that I and many others have used to find fulfilling careers. If you follow my guidance and continue taking action, you will find yourself on the right side of that statistic.

Choosing a career is one of the biggest decisions you will make in your life, if not *the* biggest. It will impact everything that you do in the future, from giving you the time you need to start a family to giving you the money you need to buy a house. It will impact your social life, your retirement age, and ultimately your happiness and health. It's not something that should be taken lightly, nor is it something you should jump into.

Read this book, spend some time on the principles discussed and make sure you give this aspect of your future the attention and the time that it deserves. There are millions of adults who look at your situation with envy and wish they could go back and do it all over again. Don't be one of those people, don't rush in and don't make the wrong decision. Be one of the successful people discussed in this book and not the unsuccessful people who wished they had read it.

Best of luck for your future and I hope you found this book useful!

FAQ

I need more help. How do I contact you?

Whether you need help with your CV, applications, job database/tracking, career advice or anything else; contact us on www.AcademicUnderdogs.com. We'll be happy to help!

We also offer mentorship programmes to help you succeed at university and beyond. Previous mentees have gone onto achieve top grades and built the confidence to impress in interviews. Using our network of employers, many of them have also been placed at fast growing start-ups around the world.

We do everything in our power to ensure you leave university with your head held high and hit the ground running as a graduate.

Do you have any other books?

Yes! *How to Land Your Dream Graduate Job* is book 3 of 3 in the *Level Up* series. Book 2, *How to be Admired & Respected*, shows you how to build a charismatic personality and influence others. Book 1, *How to ACE Your Degree,* helps undergraduates achieve top grades at university.

HOW TO BE ADMIRED & RESPECTED

From Attracting Friends to
Persuading Interviewers,
We Show You How
to Influence
Anyone

A. RAJA

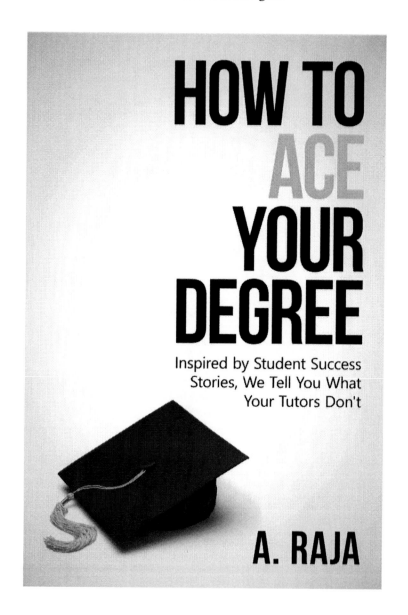

HOW TO
ACE
YOUR
DEGREE

Inspired by Student Success
Stories, We Tell You What
Your Tutors Don't

A. RAJA

Appendix 1
Conversation with Beau Jessup

"What impresses people about someone who has built a business, is that they've taken the time to do it and it's not easy. A lot of people would get bored or talk themselves out of it. It's attractive to anyone who is looking to employ you."

"That form of motivation that you've clearly had to have to create that business is applicable in many other senses, and employers want to be working with original thinkers who have displayed this motivation in the past."

"It takes strength and character to take a risk and follow it through,"

-    *Beau Jessup*

Me: *When you first came up with your idea to create a Chinese/English baby name website, what were your initial steps? How did you manage your time alongside school? Were you doing your GCSEs at the time?*

Beau: *I started thinking about it just before my GCSEs. So, I* *borrowed some money from my dad after I pitched the idea to him. That allowed me to pay to have someone host and build the site. I gave them all of my ideas, just how I wanted to want it to look. I was really adamant about being involved in the design aspect of it because I'm quite specific about the way I want things to look. Obviously, I wasn't qualified to do the coding side of things.*

Me: *Lots of developing?*

Beau: *I didn't know how to do that. I had to host it for free on another site to see if it would work, to test it out, to try out the prices and see what people were willing to pay. I started a free service. It was getting a lot of attention and people wanted it. I was like, okay, we are going to start charging for this but I then started to lose some purchases. I thought to myself, okay, it's a bit too expensive. I was just playing around with the prices for a while, and then found a price which stuck. It was about 60RMB which is the equivalent of like 60P in the UK. That pricing worked and then I paid for hosting so I had my own individual website and that's when we trans-ferred it onto its own domain.*

Me: *Was it easy to find a hosting service in China from here?*

Beau: *Yeah.*

Me: *How did you do it?*

Beau: *I had to just do some online searching. I think China is one of the hardest places to try and do business because people there have a very different approach. That became a barrier we had to get over.*

Me: *Must have been difficult at first?*

Beau: *Yes, but with these sorts of things, you just have to work through them and not let them stop you... if you keep a vision inside, everything stays on track.*

Me: *Did you invest a significant amount of money before launching the website or did you have a beta version that you put up first to see if it worked?*

Beau: *I think the only money that I spent, before the site was* *hosted on my own domain, was 1500 pounds. That's all I borrowed from my dad and as soon as I made that I paid him back.*

Me: *That was enough to get you going and the website up and for you to start testing it and playing around the prices?*

Beau: *Yeah, because I didn't do any advertisements or anything like that.*

Me: *So how did you manage to spread the word without advertising?*

Beau: *Luckily on WeChat, you can send out broadcast messages. So just have to send out tons and tons of broadcast messages, which is time consuming, but it works.*

Me: *WeChat... is that China's equivalent of WhatsApp?*

Beau: *Yeah.*

Me: *Go on...*

Beau: *WeChat coupled with word of mouth, the business spread very quickly. Also, what's good about China is that it's such a massive country. The equivalent of sales in the UK is the equivalent of like a village in China.*

Me: *Massive scale .*

Beau: *Yeah the scale is like taking the multiplier effect; it's just one mass.*

Me: *Were you working on this during term time? You thought of the idea in year nine, but then you started working year ten?*

Beau: *Yeah. It kind of started working, everything began happening around GCSE time.*

Me: *How did you manage the time? Were you revising, doing homework and then on the weekends working on this?*

Beau: *Well, luckily there was a summer holiday, which is when I did most of my 'getting the site together' and then the site was running by the time that I was back in term time.*

Me: *Okay.*

Appendix 1

Beau: *So it actually runs itself.*

Me: Because the algorithm works for you?

Beau: *Yeah, the algorithm just works itself. I didn't have to do much other than the odd bit of customer service and thinking of how I can improve the site. In terms of someone who is trying to do something during school/uni, I would say spending a certain amount of time each week or an afternoon which you always do it. Scheduling that one bit of time that you designate to it. That continuity of having that time allows things to flow steadily and you make consistent progress.*

Me: *Right.*

Beau: *Then you are not going to feel bad about losing time to revise or revision suffering at the hands of you trying to make yourself stand out by creating a business. If you schedule that time and it's always there, you are only using that time. That is your special time that you designate to your business, then you feel like you have your stuff together rather than trying to scavenger hunt for time.*

Me: *That's good advice. What's next for you?*

392

Beau: *I'm off to university in a couple of weeks.*

Me: *What are you studying?*

Beau: *I'm studying BSC social anthropology at the London School of Economics.*

Me: *What are your plans after that? Do you think you will start your own business or continue with this later?*

Beau: *I think, well, this runs itself and this is a lovely steady income. It's very easily made.*

Me: *Very passive.*

Beau: *Yeah and that's good for university life, but I don't know, I think we'll see how much I plan and if I'm really enjoying my degree I may want to utilise it more than I realise. I might even go into academics, but I would definitely like to do something that involves drawing upon what humans want, because obviously that's kind of at the core premise of my degree.*

Me: *Yeah.*

Beau: *I have quite an interest in campaign advertisement and the kind of slogans that draw people in and get people to use a company and a brand.*

Me: *So more on the marketing and branding side?*

Beau: *Yeah, because as someone who created their own company, I can see the power of advertisement and the power of a slogan, and add that and how that can actually attract people. So, using my degree to understand what it is that humans actually want will give me that kind of insider perspective in two senses.*

Me: *I think a lot with marketing and branding a word or phrase here or there can make a big difference.*

Beau: *I think that it's so interesting to see how it can have such a big influence.*

Me: *Do you have any final advice for someone who wants to start a business while studying?*

Beau: *It's just understanding that things don't go smoothly. Things just don't. It's a bit too idealistic and I think understanding that before you go into something—knowing that* *things aren't going to go perfectly—is really important. Because, when things don't go perfectly, they aren't scared off.*

Appendix 2
Conversation with Jacob Wedderburn-day

Me: *"From the moment you had the idea for City Stasher to the first customer purchase, how much time did that take?"*

Jacob: *"Three months."*

Me: *"How much did the initial site cost?*

Jacob: *"Not a lot. We originally put in 200 pounds each to buy the shares in the company. Honestly, we were probably a bit uninformed about the approach we took at the very beginning. We went away and suddenly incorporated this company when we had the original idea and then took a couple of months researching it before we actually built the prototype. The prototype website was super cheap. We used a site called ShareTribe.com. This is the advice I like giving to people. Take the MVP (minimum viable product) approach, don't go out and build a really expensive product until you've validated that it's something that people want to use. So, we spent approximately 45 pounds a month to set up this website and then set up some Google Ads for it, which were really cheap, because at the time we had no competition in this space. So yeah, it would have cost* *us about 50 quid, I think, to get our first customer through the door."*

Me: *"Did you have any competition?"*

Jacob: *"A lot of our initial research was into the self-storage space and obviously, it's quite a crowded space. It's got the big yellows and the safeguards. And then there's even newer companies like Love Space, which was relatively young at the time but still present and doing quite a good job. We weren't sure how well we could compete with all that. But we thought there is no harm in giving it a go because it was so cheap to set up. We thought this sort of platform approach lends itself much more scalability than the current kind, you know, you've got these big warehouses, they were expensive. Whereas we could get people on the website for free and so we can be a lot cheaper and charge just on commission."*

Me: *"What did you do after setting up the site?"*

Jacob: *"We had Anthony's flat on the website, then we put my flat up. We cajoled a lot of our friends and family to put their places up, which they very reluctantly did. It was through that process that we moved to the model that we currently have. We had people come to our flats and they'd drop their bags off. It was a great way to meet our customers' and ask them questions about how they found us, why they needed us, etc. We learnt that a lot of them needed storage on a much shorter-term basis than we'd predicted."*

Me: *"That's when you pivoted the business model?"*

Jacob: *"Yes, we thought we'd be a kind of self-storage alternative and actually we realised we were much more suited to being like a left-luggage alternative. People were using us because they were going to concerts, because they were going to stadiums, because they'd just been checked out in the morning and their flight was later and they didn't want to drag their bags around all day. And it was positioned so cheaply; we were half the price of the station lockers. We put a little more time and energy into researching those lockers and realised we could really compete with those. Then the next big step was to start working with shops and hotels because the flat model didn't work so well. For really short-term storage, it's quite annoying to let people in and out twice on the same day unless you're literally in your house doing nothing. Shops are open, they've got the space, they've got CCTV, they are keen to get additional revenue, same story for hotels. So, I think it was about five months after we'd originally launched, two months after our first customer that we then started signing up shops and the rest is history really."*

Me: *"Was that still at the university?"*

Jacob: *"Yes, my last year of university."*

Me: *"How did you get the first shop to sign up? Did you just walk in and pitch it to them?"*

Jacob: *"Yeah pretty much, we got rejected quite a few times before we were lucky enough to find a shop that said yes. Michelle's News Agency is right around the corner from UCL where I was studying and I was really touched when we finally had someone say yes. It took time to refine the sales pitch. The original pitch was literally, 'This is our idea but we have no traction'. We mentioned the traction that we had in our flats and we said, you know we wanted to work with shops because of the system there and we thought it would be a great way to get revenue. And I think in Michelle's case, she just found us quite cute and wanted to give us a shot! So, once you have one you can get two, once you have two, you can get four and it snowballs from there. We got a lot better at selling the idea as you start to get more traction and understand the model better anyway."*

Me: *"Did you have a system on the website for the shops where they could manage the bookings themselves?"*

Jacob: *"This is interesting. It actually took quite a long time to get right. We added a listing page for every shop and were notified by email when someone made a booking. But we had a process in the early days that they had to accept the bookings. Now it's automatic.*

In the early days we used to accept cash payments, which I think people tended to use in the beginning just because it obviously was a very new unverified website and I suppose just feels safer to pay in cash than to risk putting your credit card in. I mean not that it looked that shady, I hope!

Once the website was a bit better designed, we shifted from the cash model and that's not really been a problem since."

Me: *"So if I was in the area at the time and I wanted to store my bags at Michelle's, I would book it on the website, an email would be sent to Michelle and she would have to respond to accept. Then I would get a notification of some sort to go and drop off my bags etc; and then I pay cash to the news agent, to Michelle?"*

Jacob: *"Yeah, you'd pay cash back then."*

Me: *"And then they would just pay you a commission on each thing."*

Jacob: *Yeah, it was a bit ridiculous really, I mean we only needed about 10 shops and that's fine, but we would go around sort of like the mafia collector. Just going around to these shops with bags of money and pick up the coins."*

Me: *"Let's say back when you were storing luggage in flats, you got one or two sales, but it wasn't really picking up. What would you have done? Did you have any other business ideas in the pipeline?"*

Appendix 2

Jacob: *"Good question. When we started the process, we knew we wanted to go into business together, or we wanted to have a shot at being entrepreneurs. We talked about it loads when we were studying over that summer, it was the summer before my fourth year and it was the summer I was leaving university. So, we were like this is a great year to try something and I know London was a great place to try and start stuff too. We did brainstorm a few different ideas; to be honest the rest were pretty crap. This was the only one we felt had any real legs. I mean in some respects we were lucky that it did take off and it did start to work. I think we always felt quite strongly that it had the scale and we believed in it, so it never crossed my mind as to what we would do if it failed. But that being said, I think one of the nice things about starting as a student and not putting too much money into it... it felt like there wasn't much to lose."*

Jacob: *"Of course we did hope that it would get big enough and reach the scale where we could work on it full-time. But, we were very happy with it being just a sort of side project. There were definitely times where we thought, you know maybe that's all it would ever amount to. It was just a little thing we ran on the side, maybe made us a few hundred pounds a month. I mean, thankfully, it's gone way past that but I think if it had totally failed at some point we would have sort of recognised that, given up and gone back to the drawing board. I feel that I have a character trait where I'd love to do my own thing. I'm biased now because I've done it already for a few years and I've enjoyed it so much. So, I know that whatever I did next, I would*

402

want to go through the process again. But yeah, I guess that's how we would have dealt with it, something like that."

Me: *"You secured a graduate job at the Bank of England right? Did you mention City Stasher on your interviews or on your CV?"*

Jacob: *"I didn't at the time because the Bank of England Grad Scheme you had to apply for very early. I was going through that process before we'd even got the first site out. We had the idea but we didn't have a site. I kept it to myself, but I also didn't want to scare them with the possibility that I might jump ship and do my own thing. That being said, once it was up and running and City Stasher was starting to happen and I was about to start the scheme, I called them to say, look, I've got this project I've been working on and it's starting to look like it might be something I could commit to more and I'd love the chance to defer my place for a year and work on this. I didn't want to waste their time by taking a place. They said, no, you can't defer, see you in September basically. So in my head I was like, well, okay, I've tried. At least they know that if it does do well I'm out and I've given them the pre-warning and this is exactly what ended up happening."*

Me: *Has your experience as an entrepreneur highlighted any aptitudes that you didn't know about before?"*

Appendix 2

Jacob: *"Oh yeah. I am very grateful I didn't end up as a consultant because a lot of my friends did. It was very much a career path for people who studied economics. They work ridiculous hours. I work sometimes quite ridiculous hours, but it's not the same when it's your own thing.*

Me: *Would you ever consider going back to the corporate world?*

Jacob: *I feel like the honest answer is I wouldn't. I can't see myself really applying for the jobs in the same way. I think I'd much rather go back and try another project of my own. I'd really like to dedicate a bit more time to coding and computer science. It's not a skill-set I had before this. And I'm not one of my developers. It's something that really, really interests me. I definitely like to be in a position that I could build my own MVP from scratch next time rather than relying on third-party software. That's how I still feel about it."*

Me: *"What would you say to a current university student who is skeptical about starting a business at university?"*

Jacob: *"It is good to do these things while you're young. What I thought was fantastic about raising our first round of investment was that I felt I completely de-risked the process for myself, the worst case that would happen was the business failed and we ran out of money. I feel pretty bad about wasting someone else's money, but at least I sort of feel like I'd only be enriched by the process because I'd have this experience to sort*

404

of fall back on and take into whatever I did next. And I don't think it's an entirely sort of negative experience to fail at.

I think doing something like this demonstrates a lot of qualities. You get a lot of experience out of it, and I think future employers would actually be quite open to it. I mean I've hired people failed with start-up experiments that they've tried before and having people who have that kind of spirit is something that we look for. I'm sure other start-ups would too and probably other employees in different sort of fields. So, I wouldn't recommend wasting tons of your own money when you are young. I certainly wouldn't sort of recommend racking up debt just to run experiments like this. But if there's a way you can do it like the way we did I think it's only positive."

Me: *"Did anyone else in your year group at uni launch a business?"*

Jacob: *"Not that I really picked up on when I was at Oxford. When I moved to UCL for my Masters I got more actively involved with the Entrepreneurship Society. They had this quite cool program called the entrepreneur's challenge where we had a term running through how to develop a business idea and do a pitch."*

Me: *"There two main questions I get from students—the first one is how do I find an idea? That's the most common question I get."*

Jacob: *"Actually I have an answer for that. The idea is much less tricky than the execution. There are lots of great ideas out there. There's no formula for a good idea. What I always tell people is take a problem, look at ways of solving it and if you can do something that's cheaper, faster, or just better quality, then you've definitely got enough of an idea to start a business. Your ideas don't have to be totally original.*

If you look at the last 20 years of innovation, a lot of it is just taking existing business models and literally moving it online. So many massively successful businesses are just e-commerce versions of existing stores. E-commerce allows them to be, in many cases, cheaper, faster and better. But, I think the internet is still massively untapped and that's before you think about the applications of relatively new tech like block chain and that stuff like that."

Jacob: *"I think especially it's important if it's a problem that you've encountered yourself and you feel quite passionately about. I can't claim that luggage storage has been a lifelong passion of mine, but certainly I've been in a position where I've experienced it and it's a bit annoying. It's actually really nice that whenever we go to talks or conferences, or meet new people and explain what we do, everyone always has that moment of like, yeah, I can relate to that problem.*

There's nothing potentially brilliant about what we're doing. It was just a simple idea and the right place at the right time, there are so many other problems that you can apply the same thing to."

Me: "*As you had an interest in entrepreneurship, you seemed to have your eyes peeled for ideas.*"

Jacob: "*Yeah, that's a good point too, there's a sort of mind-set element to it. As you encounter problems you start thinking about solutions more. I feel like since starting this, we've had a lot more and a lot better ideas for foreseeable future business ventures. Now we obviously don't have any time to commit to them, but we were working on a list that we have set-up for whenever we're free and have time to put into something new.*

I think you do develop that sort of mental perspective on how you see problems in the real world and think about how you can fix them. That's all it really takes. It's just having that kind of approach."

Me: "*Did you have a lot of naysayers and people who told you it wouldn't work at the start? The second question I get asked a lot is, 'How do I stop talking myself out of trying?'*"

Jacob: "*Yes. I remember some of these conversations; how's the project going? Someone asked me that way more recently in the last year; I was like 'we've clearly been out of touch; it's a lot bigger now'. I think maybe it's an attitude thing again. I think I'm quite lucky to have such an optimistic disposition about these things. I've felt like there's so much I want to do and* *don't have enough time to do it. But I think the answer to that is really it's just about taking one step at a time."*

Jacob: *"So step one is find out more, research, look at things out there potentially competing in the space already. What competition already exists?*

Step two is: take steps toward actually executing it. We did a bit of research before we picked an idea, but then we picked it and built it. I think the most satisfying thing is to try and execute quickly really.

Step three: get some kind of test out there and once you actually have something that you're working on and it's more than just an idea, I think it's an incredibly powerful motivator. Once it's out there, you become quite proud of this thing you've created. Even if it's very early, you do feel this real sense of pride like we did with the first Citystasher.com."

Jacob: *"I think the passion never really leaves you. It's so good to take the little steps to getting up. It's much more motivating to work on something that already exists. Take it step by step is really the theme of my answer. I hope that's helpful."*